The Essence of Survival

A Guided Journey for Healing

The Essence of Survival

A Guided Journey for Healing

DR. ALLANAH ROBERTS-HEADLEY
& KEAIDY BENNETT

LEXXIKHAN PRESENTS
PUBLISHING

LexxiKhan Presents Publishing
www.LexxiKhanPresents.com

Ordering information:
Quantity sales. Special discounts are available on quantity purchases by corporations, associations, and others. For details, contact the publisher at the web address above.

This guided healing journey, provided by the publisher and author, does not guarantee specific outcomes. It is a self-help tool designed for use alongside a comprehensive healing plan and guidance from a licensed therapist or healthcare provider. Healing from trauma and personal growth are individual processes, and results may vary. This journey is intended to offer support and reflection, but professional care is strongly recommended for addressing specific needs. The publisher and author bear no responsibility for the misuse of this content. Your well-being is paramount; please seek appropriate professional guidance.

Library of Control Number 2023906561

ISBN-13: 978-1-958335-13-0 (hardcover)
　　　　　978-1-958335-14-7 (paperback)

Printed in the United States of America

DEDICATION

To all the women and men who've felt unseen and powerless—by their partner, by the world —this book is for you. It's a guide to reclaiming your true self and shedding the labels they imposed upon you. May this journey empower you and remind you of your strength, resilience, and *essence*.

Essence

noun

---

the inherent nature or indispensable characteristic of something, particularly in the abstract, that determines its fundamental nature

Survival

noun

---

the state of persistence or ongoing existence often endured despite adversity, challenges, or trying situations

The Essence of Survival

noun

---

acknowledging that your life is **indispensable** *and that* **you** *have the* **power** *to move forward and* **live**

The Doctor's Orders

The cycle of abuse is more than just a cycle; it's an addiction. From the moment we are introduced to it, the pattern unknowingly seeps into the essence of who we are. As with any other addiction, we need several things to break free and stay free from the unconscious thoughts that often lead us back into harm's way.

My name is Dr. Allanah Roberts-Headley, and I am a licensed Mental Health Counselor as well as a Counseling Educator. For the past six years, I have been working closely with patients to educate them on the different benefits of therapy and to provide counseling techniques to help them navigate their mental health challenges. While this may seem too hard to overcome at times, with some guidance and confidence, they are able to heal.

Prior to becoming a doctor or even a counselor, I was an advocate in the mental health counseling field with some background in helping domestic violence victims. I have had friends and family members who experienced this type of abuse and found it to be a very important topic to talk about and to bring more awareness to.

One of those friends has decided to co-author this book with me. Our goal is to use her transparency and my education to help you identify and break free of the unhealthy patterns that may keep someone stuck in the **cycle of abuse.**

Keaidy Bennett is a mom of three and the owner of the publishing company that produced this book you are holding. In addition to all of that, she is an activist fighting for change for domestic violence survivors. Like most survivors, Keaidy had a new set of challenges once she finally broke free from the grasp of an abusive marriage, but I'll let her explain that to you on her own.

Throughout this book, you will find information that may be triggering to you. That is because domestic violence/dating violence is not a pretty thing to work through. For this reason, I want to challenge you to open yourself up to working through this journal with a mental health therapist or counselor who can help you process the feelings that may emerge. Yes, I designed this guided journey to help you heal; however, you can accomplish more with someone else. There are multiple ways to get access to counseling. Sometimes, your health insurance may cover it, or you can reach out to local domestic violence shelters and non-profits in your area to find out if they offer free counseling or group services. Also, your employer may offer an EAP that provides you with a few free sessions to use. If you are not ready for that, I get it. How about you follow @essence_of_the_mind on Instagram so you have a way to access a healing community in the meantime?

Before we get started on our healing journey, I want us to take a moment to prepare you for what is coming next. On the next page, you will find a formal introduction from my co-author of this book. Then, after some information on safety, you will find something called a lethality assessment. Various organizations have something similar that they may ask you to complete. That is because getting out is not always the final step. In completing this assessment, please know that it is only meant to be a tool to help you and others who may be a part of your support system. It is not meant to be a stressful exercise.

I am proud of you for taking this step because it is not a small one.

Let's begin.

Dr. Allanah Roberts-Headley

FROM VICTIM TO SURVIVOR

I'm no stranger to violence. Since I was a fetus in my mother's womb, it has always had a way of showing up in my life. That is why, even when I don't try, I thrive in chaos.

In my thirty-four years of life, I have experienced almost every form of abuse and tactic that is mentioned in this guided healing journey. I stress that because I know that when you are in the thick of the storm, it can feel like you are all alone. You're not. There was once a time when I would be too embarrassed to share the things I am about to divulge with you, but I refuse to do that any longer. You see, domestic violence plays with your mind. Whether you receive a physical scar or not is irrelevant. It changes the core of who you are; your *essence* is manipulated and altered into something or someone you no longer recognize or like. Coming to that revelation was not an easy thing for me to do.

After six years together, one house, two children, and a few successful businesses, I had grown exhausted from being married to an abusive man. Sure, on the outside, my life looked like a dream. Online, I had everything a woman could ever want, but in reality, I was slowly dying. Between the fact that I had lost custody of my oldest child due to our abusive history, his infidelity, the empowered mistresses who would stop at nothing to make my life more miserable than it already was, the control he had over my body, finances, and business, I was ready to end it all. In fact, I had been having nightmares of murdering my ex-husband - because, after years of attempting to leave him, I felt like death was the only way out.

The vivid visions of me, back in an orange jumpsuit without any knowledge of what was happening to my children, gave me the mustard seed-sized faith I needed to file for divorce, finally.

"You've already lost custody of one child," he would spew whenever I suggested that we should separate. "Why do you think any judge would give you custody of my two children? The house is in my name. I'm the breadwinner, and you're crazy," he would continue. "How will you ever convince anyone other than yourself that it is in their best interest to pack them up and move to another state away from me?" While I filled out those divorce forms on my own, my mind replayed every lie he had ever thrown in my face. I cried. I prayed, and I cried some more, but I knew I didn't have the energy to pretend for another day. I was officially sick and tired of being sick and tired.

At that time, filling out that form felt like a gruesome task, so by the time I got down to the part where I had to sign and date it, I fought with myself to consider that maybe all of the things he had been saying weren't lies. Maybe they were true. Then, fortunately for me, a memory from a session I had with my therapist came to the forefront of my mind.

"Who taught you to hate yourself?" my therapist asked me in the middle of our second session that week.

"I don't hate myself," I spat back. I was shocked that he had made such a bold and *obviously* incorrect assessment of me.

"Do you think someone who genuinely loves themselves would allow someone to treat them the way you are allowing this man to treat you?"

That flashback to that virtual therapy session allowed me to remember just how long I had been dealing with domestic violence. Because I come from a culture that has a history of accepting men beating on their wives, I had been a victim before I even took my first breath. Those thoughts gave me the courage to sign my name on that divorce petition that day. I was doing it for myself, for every woman in my lineage before that couldn't, and for my children.

Filing for divorce was the easiest part. Staying out of the relationship and keeping safe was the challenge.

On my quest for freedom and rediscovering myself, I had judges tell me that they laughed at my motions. I had to live on government assistance, and I was homeless. Trust me when I tell you that I had to fight to be here. Some days, I wanted to end it all, and others, it felt easier to go back to a life that offered a little more familiarity.

I've slept in my car and have gone days without eating. I've stressed about how I would ever get back on my feet. I've felt trapped by a system that should empower and not enslave, but that is a different book for a different time. I say all of this to remind you. You are not alone, and that is why it is important for us to share our stories.

We will never heal the things we refuse to reveal, and that is why I choose to bear mine with you now. It took me three years of intense therapy to uproot thoughts and ideologies that had been projected on me by others. It took a lot of effort and intentionality to evolve into the woman I am today. This guided healing journey will be a challenge, but I pray that you will fight harder for yourself than you ever did for anyone else.

Keaidy Bennett | xo

Safety First

Our hope is that you and your children are currently in a safe environment; however, in the event that you are not, we always recommend that survivors have an emergency bag packed and ready to go.

Your emergency bag should be packed and ready for you to grab at a moment's notice. It's best to pack your bag when your abuser is not home or around and you're in a calm state. Your bag needs to be stored as safely as possible (i.e. in a closet not frequented, underneath everyday items like blankets, at a friend's house, etc. If your bag is small, or if you want to ensure a few select items are secure, consider the spare tire compartment of your car.) Below is a list of items you should consider packing, for yourself and your child/children, in your emergency bag. Please keep in mind that once you flee, you may not be able to return to the house.

Spare keys (house/car)
Driver's License
Passports/Green Cards
Birth certificate(s)
Social Security cards
Car titles
Deed to the house
Medical records
Photos to document abuse
Your diary or written log
Cash
Checks
Bank cards
Your children's important items
Your child's favorite sleep items
Jewelry
Clothes
Toiletries
Spare phone

ASSESS YOUR RISKS

Before we get started, I want you to know that this is not meant to cause you any stress or anxiety or make you relive your trauma. It is to help you better assess your current or past risk level as it pertains to domestic violence in your home.

1. Are you currently experiencing any form of physical violence or threats of physical harm?
a) Yes, frequently
b) Yes, occasionally
c) No

2. Is your abuser controlling your access to finances, resources, or basic necessities?
a) Yes, completely
b) Yes, to some extent
c) No

3. Are you currently experiencing emotional abuse, such as constant criticism, humiliation, or manipulation?
a) Yes, frequently
b) Yes, occasionally
c) No

4. Has your abuser threatened to harm you, your children, or your loved ones?
a) Yes, frequently
b) Yes, occasionally
c) No

5. Do you feel isolated from friends, family, or support networks due to the actions of your abuser?
a) Yes, frequently
b) Yes, but to some extent
c) No

ASSESS YOUR RISKS

6. Are you currently able to freely communicate with others without the presence or monitoring of your abuser?
a) No, I am constantly monitored
b) Yes, but with some restrictions
c) Yes, I have privacy in my communications

7. Has your abuser threatened you with or used a weapon such as a gun, knife, or other objects to harm you or instill fear?
a) Yes, frequently
b) Yes, occasionally
c) No

8. Have you experienced any sexual abuse or coercion within your relationship?
a) Yes, frequently
b) Yes, occasionally
c) No

9. Are you constantly monitoring your behavior and altering it to avoid triggering an abusive response?
a) Yes, constantly
b) Yes, sometimes
c) No

10. Has your abuser threatened to harm or take custody of your children if you try to leave or seek help?
a) Yes, constantly
b) Yes, occasionally
c) No

ASSESS YOUR RISKS

11. Has your abuser ever prevented you from seeking medical care and attention when you needed it?
a) Yes, frequently
b) Yes, occasionally
c) No

12. Has your abuser ever tried to manipulate or control your access to birth control or reproductive health services?
a) Yes, frequently
b) Yes, occasionally
c) No

13. Has your abuser ever threatened to "out" your sexual orientation or personal information?
a) Yes, frequently
b) Yes, occasionally
c) No

14. Does your abuser ever attempt to make you feel guilty or responsible for the abuse you've been exposed to?
a) Yes, constantly
b) Yes, sometimes
c) No

15. Has your abuser ever prevented you from pursing higher education or employment opportunities?
a) Yes, constantly
b) Yes, occasionally
c) No

ASSESS YOUR RISKS

16. Has your abuser used religious or spiritual beliefs to control or manipulate you, such as threatening to curse or invoke divine punishment if you don't comply with their demands?
a) Yes, frequently
b) Yes, occasionally
c) No

17. Do you feel a constant sense of fear or anxiety related to spiritual consequences, such as being cursed or facing harsh judgment, if you resist or leave the abusive relationship?
a) Yes, constantly
b) Yes, occasionally
c) No

18. Has your abuser coerced you into participating in religious or spiritual practices against your will, using it as a means of control or punishment?
a) Yes, frequently
b) Yes, occasionally
c) No

19. How many times have you or your children witnessed or experienced any form of abuse or manipulation?
a) Frequently (more than three times)
b) Occasionally (less than three times)
c) Never

20. How many times have you attempted to leave your abuser? (Please include times when you had to seek other accommodations because your home was not safe (i.e. sleeping in your car or staying with someone else temporarily).
a) Multiple times (more than three times)
b) A few times (less than three)
c) Once or never

ASSESS YOUR RISKS

21. Has your abuser expressed feelings of hopelessness, worthlessness, or thoughts of wanting to inflict self-harm?
a) Yes, frequently
b) Yes, occasionally
c) No

22. Are you scared that if you leave the relationship, your abuser will escalate the violence you are experiencing?
a) Yes, constantly
b) Yes, occasionally
c) No

23. Have you ever been subjected to silent treatment or isolation as a form of punishment from your abuser?
a) Yes, frequently
b) Yes, occasionally
c) No

24. Have you noticed your self-esteem or self-worth diminishing since being in this relationship?
a) Yes, significantly
b) Yes, to some extent
c) No

25. Is your abuser currently unemployed or underemployed?
a) Yes. My abuser is unemployed
b) Yes. My abuser is underemployed
c) No. My abuser is working full time

ASSESS YOUR RISKS

Now, I want you to count up the number of times you selected each letter so you can grade yourself below.

If you selected mostly (a), you may be at high risk. Your responses indicate that you are experiencing severe abuse and control, which poses a significant threat to your safety. It is crucial to reach out to a professional or local authorities for immediate assistance.

If you selected mostly (b), you may be at medium risk. Your responses suggest that you are experiencing abusive behaviors, although the level of danger may vary. Seeking support from local resources and developing a safety plan is essential to protect yourself.

If you selected mostly (c), you may be at low risk. While this does not negate the importance of seeking support and safety planning, your responses indicate a lower level of immediate danger. However, it is still vital to address the abusive dynamics in your relationship and seek assistance to ensure your ongoing safety and well-being.

Please know that this quiz is not a definitive assessment. It is meant to provide a general idea of your risk level. If you are unsure or you need further guidance, please consult with a licensed professional or consider working with a local domestic violence organization to develop a plan specifically for you.

REFLECTION

I want you to take some time and reflect on the answer you received from your risk assessment. Now, take a moment to answer these questions: how did you feel prior to starting the assessment? How did you feel during the assessment, and how do you feel now? Were your feelings the same or different? Why do you think you have these feelings? Use the space below to detail those feelings.

I AM WORTHY

Up until now, your abuser has used different tactics that have caused you to second-guess your value and purpose. This week, we want to focus on the fact that you and/or your children deserve a life that is safe and free from abuse. In fact, you deserve way more than that.

This week, we will go over safety planning and ways that you can stay safe in this season. While we talked about a lot of ways that abusers try to maintain control while you are in the relationship, we have yet to go into full detail about the things that they will try to do once you are out of that relationship.

One way that abusers attempt to maintain control is by **stalking** you. An abuser can show up at your school or place of employment. They may text or call you constantly. If you block them, they might create another account or block their number. All of these attempts are manipulative tactics to get you to believe that they are the ones that are in control. They hope that they will wear you down into submission. Your goal is to remember this fact: you are worthy of living a life that you love - one that includes safety for you and your children. You don't have to tolerate this.

Before we begin, I want to remind you that I'm proud of the progress you've made so far. While I may not know everything you've endured, I can assure you that you aren't alone in anything that has happened. Our brains have a way of convincing us that no one will ever understand. That's not true. I hope you continue to reach down inside of you. All of this work will eventually pay off. Just keep going.

Now, below this entry, I want you to jot down different ideas you may have that can help you with this challenge. Then, take a moment to consider some possible ways to put these ideas into action.

OUR SAFE WORD IS...

The purpose of the safe word is to keep you and your children safe.

Creating a safe word can be an empowering exercise to enhance safety for you and your children. Start by involving all family members in a discussion about safety and the importance of open communication. Encourage everyone to brainstorm and suggest words or phrases that can serve as a unique and memorable safe word. Once a safe word is chosen, explain its purpose as a signal to indicate that a situation is unsafe or to call for immediate help. Practice using the safe word in various scenarios, reinforcing its importance and ensuring everyone understands its meaning. Remind your children that they can use the safe word without fear of repercussions. This allows them to feel safe and heard.

For your safety, we encourage you not to write your safe word down or share it with anyone who may share it with your abuser. Once you've established your family's safe word, write down a hint (something that you will remember but will be hard for others to guess).

MY VOW OF SAFETY

Keaidy: My journey from a victim to a survivor wasn't an easy one. I wasn't prepared for just how hard it would be to rebuild my life and get to know a new version of myself. Despite the fact that I was tired of the abuse, I also never imagined my life without him. I didn't know how to do certain things without asking him first. I had relied on him to provide, and now, suddenly, I was the only one providing for a family of four. As my nervous system tried to regulate itself, I had to deal with the weight of the universe while my body barely had enough energy to survive most days. Looking back, I wish I had been a little more patient with myself as I tried to honor the vow of safety I had for myself and my family.

In the space below, I would like you to write a vow of safety to yourself. I've included something out of my own vow so I can share an example with you.

Today's Date: _____

I vow to love you in a way you have never been loved before. I will do that by not giving personal access to people who do not provide peace and safety.

I HAVE THE STRENGTH TO HEAL MY WOUNDS AND MEND MY HEART

I can and I will heal from this.

Day 1

Keaidy: I remember my first day **out**. It was nothing like I imagined. In my dreams, I had always envisioned my children and me laughing, joking, and playing. I always saw us cuddled up and enjoying our new life. Never in a million years did I imagine that I would barely have enough energy to eat something on the first day.

My ex-husband had been arrested in the middle of the night, and I spent the next few hours in a hospital while they went through all of my injuries. The police had called my only sister, and she made the forty-minute drive to pick up my three children while I was taken to the hospital. Not only did I deliver via c-section a couple of months prior, I was still facing complications and bleeding heavily. After repeating my story countless times and having to show my naked and bruised body for pictures and assessments, I didn't know how I was going to have the energy to make it through the rest of the day when it was time to return home.

I went through the rest of that day in a haze. After returning back to our 'family' home, I could only focus on the thoughts that told me he could bond out and return at any moment. Between bleeding, cooking, cleaning, changing diapers, and checking every weird sound I heard, I was exhausted. By the time I laid my head down on my pillow that night, I realized that I had gone that entire day without eating or drinking anything. Too tired and too scared to go downstairs to our kitchen, I settled on going to bed hungry.

Thankfully, I had previously spent years in therapy, so I realized what was happening. At that moment, I could have criticized myself just like my ex used to. I could have allowed myself to be defeated by guilt and shame, but I decided to use my time in therapy to my advantage.

I put my hand on my chest. I took a few deep breaths and told myself, "You're safe now." Did I feel safe? Not really, but that small act gave me authority for a moment. For just a few seconds, I felt in control of my body, something I had not felt in a while.

Today, I want you to put your hand on your chest and say, "You're safe now." Say it as many times as you need to, but give yourself permission to take back your full authority. You are not what you have been through. Believe that.

Pause & Reflect

How do you feel about completing the first day successfully?

Have you learned anything new so far?

Take a moment to write out three positive affirmations.

Day 2

Keaidy: Starting over can seem scary. However, I would like to challenge you with this perspective switch. Instead of looking at it as a bad thing, is it possible that this moment is just a chance for you to begin again, only this time with more knowledge? 'Cause let me tell you - that's what it was for me. Using the space below, I want you to take a moment to dream. What new things can you do now that you are no longer living with someone who tries to control you? What new experiences are you looking forward to the most?

The experiences I'm looking forward to the most are....

I AM NOT A VICTIM.

I will survive & thrive.

Day 3

In order to embark on a journey of healing, it is crucial to understand the nature and extent of the abuse that has affected your life. Today, we are going to dive into the definition of **abuse** as we slowly learn more about the various forms. By shedding light on these different types of abuse, my goal is to help you recognize the patterns and effects they have had on your well-being and the well-being of any children involved.

Abuse is any action that causes harm or injury to another person. Abuse can manifest in different ways. These include physical, sexual, psychological, emotional, spiritual, financial, and reproductive coercion. Before we define each type, let's write down your definition of abuse so you can compare how your views may differ.

What is your definition of abuse? Does it differ from the definition above?

Without looking ahead, can you list some of the forms of abuse that you or your children have suffered through?

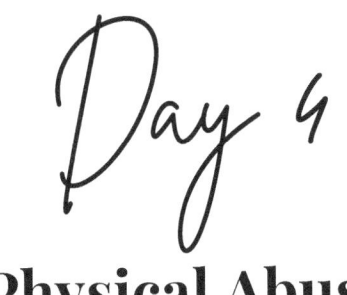

Physical Abuse

Physical abuse is the most visible and recognizable form of abuse. It involves the use of physical force to inflict harm, pain, or injury upon another person. It may show up as hitting, slapping, punching, kicking, strangling, or any other act that causes bodily harm. The scars of physical abuse extend far beyond the physical and what we see. While the scars will eventually heal, physical abuse can leave a deep emotional and psychological wound.

Today, let's spend some time learning more about physical abuse and the impacts that it has on you, your body, and those around you.

Recognizing Physical Abuse

Physical abuse does not always leave a mark; however, it is important to recognize certain signs and how they can be showing in your life or the lives of those you love. These include but are not limited to:

- recurrent bruises and black eyes
- raised welts
- burn marks
- large wounds
- broken bones
- untreated injuries in various stages of healing
- unexplained scratches
- high dosage of medications in your lab work
- someone reporting that they have been physically abused
- a sudden change in behavior
- the abuser's refusal to allow visitors to see a vulnerable adult alone

Short-Term Effects of Physical Abuse

The short-term effects of physical abuse can range from minor injuries to potentially life-altering injuries.

Impact on Children

It is super important to acknowledge that physical abuse affects not only you - the survivor - but also your children who may have witnessed or experienced it. Children exposed to violence in the home may develop emotional and behavioral problems, experience difficulties in school, and have an increased risk of perpetuating or experiencing abuse later in life. Breaking the cycle of violence is crucial to your well-being and the future leaders that you are raising.

Short-Term Effects of Impacts on Children Who Witness Physical Abuse

In the short term, children who witness domestic violence may display a wide range of emotional and behavioral reactions to life and those around them. These can include:

- fear & anxiety
- emotional distress
- behavioral changes
- relationship difficulties
- nightmares/night terrors
- academic challenges
- issues with self-worth and identity

Long-Term Effects of Children Who Witness Physical Abuse

In the long-term, children who witness domestic violence may display a wide range of concerns when it comes to the way they respond to the world around them as they continue to grow. These can include:

- emotional and mental health issues
- interpersonal challenges (This is a fancy way of saying that children may struggle to develop and maintain healthy relationships. Those who suffer in this area typically have issues with trust, intimacy, and establishing/maintaining boundaries. In fact, they may even repeat unhealthy patterns they swore never to repeat.)

- academic and career challenges
- continuation of the cycle (Our children won't always listen to what we tell them to do; however, there is a better chance that they will mimic the example we've set.)

Essence of Survival

We do not have to repeat cycles because we have grown comfortable with them. Our children do not have to repeat the cycles they may have been exposed to. **We have the power to stand up today and say, "No more."** With the right support, intervention, and healing opportunities, you can break free and build a life that you love to live.

In this section, I intentionally did not list the long-term impacts of physical abuse. That is because the truth can be hard to accept. Some victims never get out. Some victims have to live with physical scars and alterations to their bodies as a result of what they've been through. Survivors may struggle with mental health challenges or flashbacks of the abuse.

Today, I want you to answer the following questions in the box below. Then, take a moment to reflect on what you've learned.

- **What are the short-term physical effects of physical violence?**
- **What are some long-term physical effects?**
- **What are the mental health effects of physical abuse?**

_____

Pause & Reflect

What did you learn about physical abuse?

How do you think this will help you move forward in a positive way?

Day 5

If you've had to witness domestic violence, then you know that it leaves more than just physical damage. In fact, it can also impact those who were not the intended victim or target.

Today, I want you to reflect back on your first experience with physical abuse. If you haven't been a victim, how do you think you would feel if you had to witness it?

I would describe my first experience of physical abuse as...

Day 6

For these next few pages, we are going to spend some time organizing the thoughts going on in your head. Right now, you are understandably going through a lot. You may be in the process of transitioning from a stay-at-home parent to one that needs to work again. You may be in the process of relocating. Maybe your children had to change routines as a result of what has gone on. Going through all of those changes without a plan can leave you feeling like you are on a never-ending rat race. Let's organize those thoughts by getting them out.

The thoughts that keep replaying in my head the most are...

What tasks need to be handled today?

What tasks need to be completed before the end of this week?

What tasks need to be completed within this month?

Is there a simple task that I can do right now?

Using the information from the previous pages, fill out the boxes below. Then work to complete the tasks that you need to. For this first box, I want you to find a motivational quote that will help you through this week. Write it down below.

MOST IMPORTANT   CAN WAIT...   URGENT

PROJECTS THAT ARE NOT   PROJECTS I CAN ASK FOR
MINE TO WORRY ABOUT   HELP WITH

Day 7

This week, we really dug deep, and I'm so proud of you. You learned about physical abuse and did a brain dump to help you re-organize your new life.

For this exercise, I want you to answer this guided journal prompt. This exercise is meant to get you to dig deeper. If you feel like you need more space, please grab another sheet of paper and continue to express yourself.

Maintaining an abusive relationship has cost me so much. The hardest sacrifice I've made has been...

MY PAST IS NOT A REFLECTION OF MY FUTURE

I am evolving & growing.

Sexual Abuse

Keaidy: Today, let's talk about something really tough but important: sexual abuse. As a survivor, I've wrestled with the idea that what happened to me was somehow my fault. It took me a long time to accept that it wasn't.

Sexual abuse is when someone does something to your body you did not consent or agree to. This can be things like removing a condom in the middle of sex, touching you after you've already said no, or even physically forcing themselves onto you. All of these things are not ok.

Like I did, victims will often blame themselves for what happened, but please hear me when I say this: it was not your fault. It was never your fault. It doesn't matter what you wore, who you were with, if you had a couple of drinks first, or even the fact that you originally consented and then changed your mind. Your no has power whether that person honored it or not.

I have had to process the difficult feelings and emotions that come with healing from this part of the journey, but it is absolutely worth it on the other side.

Let's get ready to learn more about sexual abuse and its impacts, but more importantly, let's get ready to do some life-changing work on our healing journey. You got this.

Recognizing Sexual Abuse

If you are a sexual abuse survivor, you often face challenges in recognizing and acknowledging the abuse you have gone through. It is very common for survivors to feel shame, guilt, and self-blame. In learning how to recognize the signs, you can begin to break free from the shame and guilt that you were never meant to carry. Common signs of sexual abuse include:

- unexplained physical injuries in the genital or anal areas
- changes in behavior (withdrawal, aggression, excessive fear)
- emotional challenges (depression, anxiety, self-destructive behaviors)
- unexplained venereal diseases

- ripped, torn, or bloody undergarments
- difficulty forming trusting relationships by displaying inappropriate sexual boundaries

Short-Term Effects of Sexual Abuse

The short-term effects of sexual abuse can range from minor injuries to emotional distress, sleep disturbances (nightmares or other sleep-related issues), difficulty concentrating, memory problems, changes in eating patterns, and a change in your self-esteem and body image.

Long-Term Effects of Sexual Abuse

The effects of sexual abuse can persist long after the abuse has ended. Survivors may experience a range of long-term consequences, including:

- post-traumatic stress disorder (PTSD)
- sexual difficulties (fear of intimacy, engaging in self-destructive sexual behaviors)
- emotional and mental health issues
- negative self-image, self-blame, and a distorted sense of self-worth

Impact on Children

Children who experience or witness sexual abuse endure immense pain and suffering, both in the short term and throughout their lives. Their innocence is shattered, and the effects of this violation can shape their emotional, cognitive, and social development in unhealthy ways.

Short-Term Effects of Children Who Witness or Experience Sexual Abuse

In the short-term, children can experience:

- emotional and mental health issues
- behavioral changes
- unexplained pain, discomfort, or injuries
- regression (some children may regress in their developmental milestones and revert back to behaviors they have outgrown)

Long-Term Effects of Children Who Witness or Experience Sexual Abuse

In the long term, they can experience:

- psychological and emotional challenges
- sexual and relationship difficulties
- education and career challenges
- they can possibly repeat the cycle of abuse

Essence of Survival

If you've survived sexual abuse, you deserve compassion, support, and a path toward healing. I wish I could wrap my arms around you and let you know that I'm sorry you've experienced what you've endured. I wish the people before would have handled you with more care and appreciation.

In the space provided, I want you to take a moment to sympathize with yourself and your situation. Take a moment to say to yourself what you wish someone else would have said to you. (If this section does not apply to you, then use the space provided to explain sexual abuse to someone unfamiliar with it.)

Pause & Reflect

What did you learn about sexual abuse?

How do you think this will help you move forward in a positive way?

Day 9

Yesterday, we learned a lot about sexual abuse and the impacts that it can have on the victim as well as children that have to witness or experience it.

Today, I want you to take a moment to reflect back on what you learned. Then, I want you to take a minute and imagine that you are comforting a friend who has recently gone through it. What would you say to him/her? How would you comfort your friend in their time of need?

I AM WORTHY OF LOVE, RESPECT, AND KINDNESS.

I do not have to perform in order to receive love.

Psychological Abuse

Psychological abuse is also known as mental or verbal abuse. It is characterized by the use of words, actions, or behaviors that manipulate, control, degrade, or make you question your self-worth. Psychological abuse can manifest through constant criticism, humiliation, gaslighting, threats, intimidation, and isolation. This insidious form of abuse leaves invisible scars, eroding one's self-esteem, confidence, and mental well-being.

Today, we will explore the ugly nature of psychological abuse. My hope is to shed light on its destructive impact on survivors. By understanding the signs and effects of psychological abuse, we can empower ourselves to break free from its grip and embark on a journey of healing and self-empowerment.

Recognizing Psychological Abuse

Psychological abuse involves the use of manipulation, coercion, and power/control to sabotage your sense of self-worth and security. It often includes tactics like gaslighting, humiliation, intimidation, and isolation. In addition, other signs may include:

- calling you insulting names or making comments about your weight
- questioning your memory or events or denying things that you have witnessed or have proof of
- acting jealous and constantly accusing you of cheating
- threatening to hurt themselves, pets, or those that you love and care for
- changing the subject whenever you try to talk about your feelings
- dismissing the feelings you have by saying that you are being dramatic

Short-Term Effects of Psychological Abuse

The short-term effects of psychological abuse can include:

- emotional distress
- self-esteem issues

- isolation
- cognitive confusion (gaslighting and manipulation can cause you to doubt your reality, memory, and perception. This can cause you to struggle with decision-making and second-guessing yourself.)

Long-Term Effects of Psychological Abuse

The effects of psychological abuse can linger long after the abuse has ended. Long-term effects can include but are not limited to:

- emotional and psychological trauma (for example, you may suffer from PTSD, depression, or another type of anxiety disorder)
- issues with self-identity
- difficulty trusting yourself and others
- intergenerational trauma (this is a fancy way of saying that whatever you do not heal from, you can pass on to your children)

Impact on Children

Children who experience or witness psychological abuse within their home life will face a lot of challenges as they may grow up having a hard time identifying their reality.

Short-Term Effects of Children Who Witness or Experience Psychological Abuse

In the short term, children can experience:

- emotional and mental health issues
- behavioral changes

Long-Term Effects of Children Who Witness or Experience Psychological Abuse

In the long term, they can experience:

- psychological and emotional challenges
- interpersonal challenges

- they can possibly repeat the cycle of abuse

Keaidy's Two Cents

Psychological abuse is literally a war of your mind. I once found my ex-husband cheating, and would you believe that he deleted the messages in front of me and then tried to convince me that I had imagined the entire thing? Because I had no immediate plans to leave him, I eventually had to act as if the incident had never happened; however, it empowered me to start creating notes for myself because I could not always trust his account of an incident.

On my journey to healing, I had to be committed to my journal entries. It was one of the tools that helped empower me to leave and stay out. Having a daily account of the things that happened put things in a new perspective for me and helped me to see that I was not as crazy as he tried to make me feel.

Essence of Survival

You are worthy of love, respect, and a life free from psychological abuse. For this next exercise, I want you to write out any personal examples you have of psychological abuse. If you have not suffered from that, then how would you explain it to someone who has never dealt with it before?

Pause & Reflect

What did you learn about psychological abuse?

How do you think this will help you move forward in a positive way?

Day 11

Yesterday, we unpacked the very difficult topic of psychological abuse. Today, I want you to reflect on what you've learned, but I also want you to take a moment to consider how you may have been subjected to it in the past.

If you've been a victim, I want you to write about your first experience. If you have not experienced this, how do you plan to protect yourself now that you have more information about it?

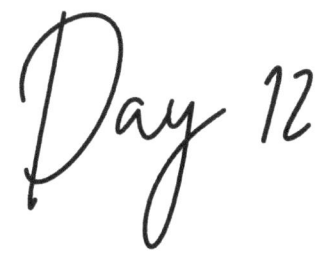

Day 12

Abusive relationships cost us a lot. For this exercise, I want you to list ten things that you've lost due to your past abusive relationship on the left, and then on the right, I want you to list how you plan on getting those things back.

Things I lost...	Plan to get it back...

I know that as you transition to your new life, your brain is going to try to convince you that it wasn't that bad where you were before. Please understand that while those thoughts may come, it does not mean that it is true. This exercise is meant to remind you of all of the things you had to sacrifice to get here.

Day 13

Today, I want you to spend some time getting familiar with domestic violence facts and statistics. Use the space below to answer the following questions. Instead of writing a simple answer for each question, use the information you've received to explain the facts as if you were explaining them to someone who did not know about domestic violence.

1. How many women are abused every minute in the United States?
2. How many women and children are homeless in America because of domestic violence?
3. What is the percentage of abuse victims that also deal with financial abuse?
4. How often (on average) does a victim return to their abuser?
5. What is the percentage of children who report experiencing domestic violence?
6. How many men, on average, are victims of domestic violence?
7. Why don't men typically report domestic violence?

Day 14

You are two weeks down! Congratulations. You made a commitment to yourself, and you are seeing that through. You should be proud of yourself.

Today, I want you to take a moment to reflect on what you've learned about yourself over these last fourteen days. How is this version of you different than the version that existed a couple of weeks ago?

Therapy

noun

---

guided support by a licensed professional to help you heal and return to the essence of who you were created to be

Emotional Abuse

Emotional abuse is meant to be an attack on your feelings and emotions. Your abuser will expose your vulnerabilities so they can maintain power and control. This can show up as consistent invalidation of your feelings, constant humiliation, and the manipulation of your emotions to create dependency and fear. Emotional abuse can result in long-lasting trauma, impacting your self-image, relationships, and ability to trust yourself and others.

Recognizing Emotional Abuse

Emotional abuse involves the consistent and subtle use of words, actions, and behaviors to undermine your sense of self, self-esteem, and emotional well-being. It is characterized by tactics such as constant criticism, humiliation, manipulation, silent treatment, and belittlement. Emotional abuse can be just as damaging as physical or sexual abuse, leaving wounds that require work to heal. Signs of emotional abuse can include:

- being extremely withdrawn and non-communicative
- unusual behavior (like rocking, biting, or sucking)
- nervousness
- the abuser will openly humiliate you

Short-Term Effects of Emotional Abuse

The short-term effects of emotional abuse can be devastating. Some common short-term effects include (but are not limited to):

- low self-esteem
- anxiety and fear
- emotional instability (Emotional abuse can cause you to experience intense mood swings, including sadness, anger, and despair. A survivor can live their life on eggshells, trying to appease an abuser's ever-changing expectations.)
- social isolation

Long-Term Effects of Emotional Abuse

Long-term effects of emotional abuse can include but are not limited to:

- Complex Post-Traumatic Stress Disorder (Long story short, emotional abuse can result in a type of complex trauma that encompasses a range of emotional, psychological, and relational difficulties.
- self-trust and issues implementing boundaries
- negative self-image
- intergenerational trauma (this is a fancy way of saying that whatever you do not heal from, you can pass on to your children.)

Impact on Children

Children who experience or witness emotional abuse within their home life will face a unique set of challenges and long-term consequences.

Short-Term Effects of Children Who Witness or Experience Emotional Abuse

In the short term, children can experience the following:

- emotional distress
- behavioral changes

Long-Term Effects of Children Who Witness or Experience Emotional Abuse

In the long term, they can experience:

- psychological and emotional challenges
- interpersonal challenges

Keaidy's Two Cents

It's incredibly difficult to maneuver through this world if you don't trust your own voice or intuition. When an abuser can get us to doubt ourselves, we are left wide open to believe anything they tell us. If we are not intentional, our inner dialogue will begin to mirror what we hear from our abusers.

Growing up, I used to hear the phrase, "It starts at home," a lot. This means that certain patterns develop in the place we should feel the safest. In my experience as a survivor and working with other survivors, a lot of us became comfortable with the abuse we endured from emotionally unsafe caretakers. Their words were harsh, demanding, and demeaning. Before most of us ever had the opportunity to know, accept, or love ourselves, we had begun to see ourselves through the lens of someone abusing us. Whether it was done intentionally or not is irrelevant; emotional abuse changes the way you see yourself and the world around you.

The day my therapist confronted me with the question, "Who taught you to hate yourself," is the same day that he gave me some hard lessons that took me months to learn. **If you don't see the problem where the cycle begins, the abuse will continue.** Do you know where it started? Can you think of who planted the seeds in your mind to accept less than you deserve?

Essence of Survival

Regardless of the lies your abuser has told you, you have an inner strength and resilience that can help you heal and transform. From this moment forward, you can implement tools to help you heal and set healthy boundaries. This can include attending therapy or group counseling sessions. Believe it or not, therapy is not just about discussing your past. Instead, therapy is a great way to help you identify patterns that have you stuck while creating a healing plan to help you move forward.

Today, I want you to write out a core value. A core value is something that is true about you all the time. Keaidy will write an example to get you started

---

I honor my boundaries with every relationship I have.

Pause & Reflect

What did you learn about emotional abuse?

How do you think this will help you move forward in a positive way?

I AM WORTH IT.

I AM AT PEACE WITH WHO I AM, & I EMBRACE MY TRUE SELF.

I am worthy of the love I give to others.

Day 16

Emotional and psychological abuse can appear very similar, but I intentionally listed them as two different forms of abuse because they are.

I want you to take a moment to reflect back on your past experiences with emotional abuse. How would you describe that experience to someone who has never been through it? If you've never experienced it, how would you encourage someone you know?

Psychological vs. Emotional

Let's take a moment to review the similarities and differences of psychological and emotional abuse.

Similarities

- **Non-physical**: Both forms do not leave a physical mark. Instead, they go for your mental and emotional well-being.
- **Manipulation:** Both forms require manipulation from the abuser. This is how they are able to get you to question your worth, purpose, and even your sanity.
- **Isolation:** Abusers need to get you alone in order for their manipulation tactics to work best. They create drama and damage your reputation with those you love, so you don't have anyone else but them to rely on.
- **Damage to Self-Esteem:** Both forms have a goal to get you to question your value. This is to keep you in your position. They do this so you won't realize your value and leave them one day.

Differences

- **Focus:** Both forms have a different focus. Psychological abuse is done to make you feel powerless and crazy. Emotional abuse is to play on your emotional well-being while diminishing your self-esteem.
- **Tactics:** While they both use manipulation, psychological abuse can include tactics like brainwashing and gaslighting. Emotional abuse includes a lot of guilt-tripping and name-calling.
- **Legal Recognition:** In some states and jurisdictions, psychological abuse may be legally recognized as a form of abuse. Emotional abuse may not always be recognized the same way.
- **End Goal:** The end goal for psychological abuse is to control the victim's thoughts, beliefs and behaviors. Emotional abuse aims to control the way you see yourself.

Day 17

Being trapped in an abusive relationship can seriously cap our ability to dream big for ourselves. Today, I want you to write ten things you look forward to in this new season.

_____

1.

2.

3.

4.

5.

6.

7.

8.

9.

10.

Spiritual/Cultural Abuse

Spiritual/Cultural abuse is a form of manipulation that targets your beliefs, religious or spiritual practices, and values. Abusers will use religious, cultural, or spiritual ideas to show power, instill fear, or justify abusive behaviors. Spiritual abuse can lead to a profound sense of confusion, lack of faith, and a disconnection with your spirituality.

Recognizing Spiritual/Cultural Abuse

Spiritual abuse involves the misuse of religious, cultural, or spiritual beliefs and practices to exert control, manipulate, and harm you. This can show up in forced beliefs and using spiritual teachings as a means of domination. Signs may include:

- using scripture or practices to humiliate you
- manipulating scripture or practices to force you into sex or submission
- coercing you into donating money to sources you really don't want to
- justifying his/her cheating behavior with scripture or religious practices that you don't want to be a part of
- using scripture or religious practices to expose your shortcomings. Abuser only identifies with the parts that glorify or magnify the abuser.

Short-Term Effects of Spiritual/Cultural Abuse

The short-term effects of spiritual/cultural abuse can be challenging to navigate alone. Some common short-term effects include (but are not limited to):

- confusion and doubt (After a while, you will feel like you've lost yourself, your purpose, and your place in this universe. You'll question how 'real' you are and what you truly believe in.)
- guilt and shame (I could write a book about these two things, but we'll save it for another day. All I want is for you to remember this: those two bags are heavy and will drag you down if you **allow** them to.)
- loss of faith

Long-Term Effects of Spiritual/Cultural Abuse

The long-term effects of spiritual/cultural abuse can cause you to lose yourself and stunt your spiritual growth. Some common long-term effects include but are not limited to:

- spiritual trauma (This type of abuse causes a disruption in your connection to your spirituality, higher power, or inner self. This can lead to hopelessness, emptiness, and even despair.)
- identity crisis (It may be hard to reconcile who your abuser has painted you to be and who you are.)
- fear of spirituality (Abusers can threaten curses and hexes on you and everything you love.)

Impact on Children

Children who experience or witness spiritual abuse within their home life will grow up having a distorted idea of reality and themselves.

Short-Term Effects of Children Who Witness or Experience Spiritual Abuse

In the short-term, children can experience:

- emotional distress
- behavioral changes

Long-Term Effects of Children Who Witness or Experience Spiritual Abuse

In the long term, they can experience:

- psychological and emotional challenges
- interpersonal challenges
- spiritual disconnection (They may struggle to identify what they should believe in.)
- loss of trust

Essence of Survival

Spiritual/cultural abuse can be a tricky space to navigate. I want to encourage you to use the space below to find a creative way to share that experience and get it off of your chest. You can write a letter to yourself, create a poem, or even write a short story.

Pause & Reflect

What did you learn about spiritual/cultural abuse?

How do you think this will help you move forward in a positive way?

Day 19

Keaidy: Yesterday, you learned about spiritual/cultural abuse. Today, I want to add to that.

Cultural abuse, like a lot of these other abuse types, tends to start at home. I was originally born in Honduras, so that means in my culture, it is normal to expect a certain level of disrespect from your elders. Because certain abuse tactics are so ingrained into a culture, others don't see it as a problem, but it is.

In business, I've learned that one of the most dangerous expressions we can use is, "It has always been done this way." The same is true for some of the things that we have culturally accepted.

Today, I want you to take a moment to write down and reflect on how spiritual/cultural abuse has shown up in your own life. Be as detailed as you need to be.

Day 20

Starting over is difficult for us as adults, so it can be very scary for children. For this exercise, I want you to list out the differences you've noticed in your child (or children) since you've taken the steps to transition to a safer way of living.

If you do not have children, use the space below to describe things that you think a child will struggle with as they adjust to a new life.

Day 21

Congratulations! You are three weeks into safer living, I hope you are proud of yourself for seeing this through.

In the boxes below, take a moment to answer each question. Be honest with yourself as you reflect on your journey. Trust me it helps.

Did you put your all into your daily activities?   **YES   NO**
No matter how you feel about your answer, take a moment to use the space below to explain why you answered your question the way you did.

Do you feel proud of yourself for the effort you put in? **YES   NO**
Again, take a moment to reflect on why.

Has it been easy to commit to your vow of safety?   **YES   NO**
If you answered yes, can you reflect on some things that have helped you? If you answered no, then how do you plan to honor the commitment you made to yourself?

On a scale from 1-10 (with 1 being the lowest and 10 being the highest), what would you grade yourself in the area of self-confidence? Why?

What are some things you can do to change the way that you view yourself?

Do you need to make any changes to your daily habits to ensure a better review next time?   **YES   NO**

On a scale from 1-10, what would you grade yourself so far? Why?

What are some changes you are willing to make to have a better review next time?

Financial Abuse

Financial abuse is a tactic used by abusers to keep you trapped and fully dependent on them. This can make leaving and staying gone feel like an impossible task.

Recognizing Financial Abuse

Financial abuse is a way an abuser trains you to rely on them fully. This is done by limiting your access to financial resources and controlling your finances. This can often look like:

- limiting your access to money (even money you've earned)
- sabotaging your employment opportunities (Abusers can do this by forcing you to be late by withholding your keys or threatening violence or harm. Abusers may also stalk you at work or start fights at your place of employment.)
- accumulating debt in your name without your consent
- draining your savings
- taking your money without permission
- forcing you to do things you do not want to do in exchange for money that they control (prostitution and pimping)

Short-Term Effects of Financial Abuse:

The short-term effects of financial abuse can be felt immediately. This can leave you feeling trapped and dependent on your abuser. Some common short-term effects include:

- financial instability (this can leave you feeling hopeless or limit your options for leaving)
- emotional distress
- isolation (Abusers often use financial control as a means of isolating you from your support network. This can make it difficult to seek assistance or find alternative housing and employment. This can intensify your feelings of dependency and vulnerability.
- loss of personal property as the abuser will sell, give away, or pawn your items
- damage to your credit score
- evictions (this makes it harder to rent future places without the abuser)
- dcbt accumulation

Long-Term Effects of Financial Abuse

The long-term effects of financial abuse can have a lasting impact on you and your children. Some common long-term consequences can include:

- financial dependency
- debt and credit issues
- limited career and educational opportunities (Financial abuse may restrict you from pursuing education or career advancements. Limited access to resources and opportunities can hinder your ability to achieve financial independence and reach your full potential.)

Impact on Children

Children who experience financial abuse may face challenges from a lack of resources to homelessness. Children may also suffer some long-term consequences from experiencing so many challenges at a vulnerable age.

Short-Term Effects of Children Who Witness or Experience Financial Abuse

In the short term, children can experience the following:

- emotional distress
- instability and uncertainty (Financial abuse can disrupt a child's stability and the security of their life.)

Long-Term Effects of Children Who Witness or Experience Financial Abuse

In the long term, they can experience:

- financial literacy and independence issues (Children who have experienced financial abuse may lack the necessary skills and knowledge to manage their finances effectively. They may require support and education to develop financial literacy and independence.)
- Career limitations (Financial abuse can hinder children's career opportunities and educational pursuits. They may not have the self-esteem and self-reliance to pursue their passions or higher education. This can impact their long-term financial opportunities.

Keaidy's Two Cents

Financial abuse is a sneaky one. I worked for a well-known investment bank, and not even the financial industry provided me with the resources I needed. There were no programs or organizations to validate that I was going through financial abuse, so I didn't have anyone I felt comfortable sharing just how bad it had gotten.

We can't heal what we won't reveal. I've also done some things I'm not proud of just to *survive*. But the first step out of survival mode, for me, was in my mind. I had to accept that I was not defined by the moment I was going through. I settled in my heart that I was only in a difficult season, and *this too shall pass*. It wasn't easy, and I had to challenge thoughts that constantly came against that. But it was work that needed to be done.

There are organizations out there that can help you develop a budget. Some non-profits can help you get into a place of your own and pay your rent for a set amount of time. If you find yourself too overwhelmed with everything, you can ask about case management from your local domestic violence organization. They can help you create a plan and work with you to accomplish your goals.

Essence of Survival

Keaidy: While your current situation may not be ideal, this moment does not define you. While there may be difficult days and nights ahead of you, this transition is birthing a version of you that you've never met before. Be gentle with him/her. Right now, you deserve that most. Using the space below, I'm going to challenge you to do something that I used to have my children do when they struggled to understand certain expectations. I want you to write the following sentence at least three times.

I am not my current financial situation. Better days are coming.

Pause & Reflect

What did you learn about financial abuse?

How do you think this will help you move forward in a positive way?

Day 23

Yesterday, you learned about financial abuse. Now, I want you to take a moment to reflect on how financial abuse may have happened to you.

Today, I want you to take a moment to write down how financial abuse has shown up in your own life. Be as detailed as you need to be.

I LOVE MYSELF AND MY LIFE.

I RELEASE THE WEIGHT OF MY PAST AND I EMBRACE A BRIGHTER FUTURE

Healing is my birthright.

Day 24

So far, we have covered a lot of information about the different ways that abuse can be manifested.

Today, I want you to take a moment to write a letter to your younger self. What would you say to him/her? Would you offer any warnings? Why or why not?

Reproductive Coercion

Reproductive coercion is a form of abuse that specifically targets your reproductive choices, body, and integrity. It involves the use of control, manipulation, and intimidation tactics to interfere with your reproductive health decisions. Reproductive coercion can look like sabotaging your birth control, forcing you to get pregnant, or even forcing a miscarriage. Abusers use these tactics to force you into motherhood or strip your right to it.

Recognizing Reproductive Coercion

Reproductive coercion requires manipulation, control, forced beliefs, and sex in an effort to control your body and your right to reproduce. Signs of reproductive coercion include:

- abuser threatens to harm you if you use birth control
- abuser forces you into sex with the intent of impregnating you
- abuser removes a condom during sex without your consent, which can result in unwanted pregnancies or expose you to sexually transmitted diseases
- abuser threatens harm, violence, removal of love or financial resources if you don't consent to an abortion

Short-Term Effects of Reproductive Coercion:

The short-term effects of reproductive coercion can be felt immediately and can be quite overwhelming. This can leave you feeling trapped and dependent on your abuser. Some common short-term effects include:

- physical and emotional trauma (You may experience injury during forced sexual acts. You may also suffer a range of emotions, from rage, guilt, and shame to pleasure. This can disrupt your sense of safety and lead to emotional distress.)
- self-blame and guilt (Your brain is going to try to convince you that this is your fault. Do not listen to those thoughts. It doesn't matter what you said, did, or wore that day. This is not your fault.)
- trust issues (Sexual coercion can shatter your trust in others and yourself. This can make

- (continued) it difficult to form intimate relationships or feel safe in vulnerable situations.)

Long-Term Effects of Sexual Coercion

The long-term effects can deeply impact your quality of life. Some of the common long-term effects include (but are not limited to):

- Post Traumatic Stress Disorder
- Sexual Dysfunction and Intimacy Issues (You may struggle to have arousal in situations that do not involve humiliation or some degradation. That is why it is important to begin a healing journey that supports you in reclaiming a positive and healthy relationship with yourself and your sexuality.)
- emotional and mental health challenges
- unwanted pregnancies
- untreatable sexual transmitted diseases

Impact on Children

Children who witness or experience sexual coercion within their families will face many struggles and challenges.

Short-Term Effects of Children Who Witness or Experience Sexual Coercion

In the short term, they can experience:

- Confusion and Fear - Children may experience confusion and fear as they struggle to understand appropriate boundaries and inappropriate actions. This can lead to a sense of vulnerability and anxiety.
- Emotional Distress - Witnessing or experiencing sexual coercion can lead to children feeling guilt, shame, and confusion. They may struggle with their sexuality and face difficulties forming healthy relationships in the future.
- Financial Challenges - Unwanted pregnancies can leave resources limited. The child can lack resources from food to housing.

Long-Term Effects of Children Who Witness or Experience Sexual Coercion

The long-term effects can deeply impact a child's way of living. Some of the common long-term effects include (but are not limited to):

- Impact on Relationships - Children may struggle to form healthy relationships after being exposed to toxic or unhealthy manipulation tactics. They may also struggle with expressing their needs and developing a positive self-image.

- Psychological and Emotional Challenges - Children may carry emotional scars of sexual coercion into adulthood. They can experience things like depression, anxiety, post-traumatic stress, and self-destructive behaviors.

Essence of Survival

Whether you are already living with the consequences of sexual coercion or just learning about it, you can now do something to change it moving forward. Your body is your own, and you should feel confident in that decision. In the space below, I want you to write a letter to your younger self. With what you now know, what advice would you give yourself after your first experience with sexual coercion?

Pause & Reflect

What did you learn about reproductive coercion?

How do you think this will help you move forward in a positive way?

Day 26

Yesterday, we had a chance to dive deep into reproductive coercion and how to recognize some of the signs.

Today, I want you to take a moment to reflect on your experience with reproductive coercion. Have you experienced this type of abuse before? If you have, take a moment to write about your first experience. If you have not, what would you say to someone who has been a victim?

Day 27

Today, please take a moment to reflect on how you've had to become a better advocate for yourself through this process.

Using the space below, I want you to list the times you've recently had to speak up for yourself more than you typically would have. How did it make you feel?

Day 28

When I was working on the contents of this book, I wanted to make sure that I didn't miss a single version of domestic violence. Today, I want to spend some time talking about how abusers may use your children to attack you.

Because children are often very impressionable and forgiving, abusers may use your own children as pawns. This can look like:

- An abuser may tell the children that you are crazy.
- An abuser may tell the children that you are the problem and the reason your family is not together anymore.
- Abusers may limit your time with the children or threaten to take you to court so they will have full custody.

Having this information, what would you say to someone who is having to deal with this tactic of abuse? Use the box below.

Day 29

The 'Silent Knight' abuse tactic, also known as the silent treatment or stonewalling, is a manipulative tactic used by abusers to exert control and power over their victims. This form of abuse involves intentionally shutting down communication and emotionally withdrawing as a means of punishment or control. Here are some signs to help you recognize 'Silent Knight' abuse:

- Emotional Withdrawl - The abuser consistently avoids communication, integration, and emotional connection. They may give you the cold shoulder, refuse to speak, become unresponsive, leaving you feeling ignored and isolated.

- Extended Periods of Silence - The silent treatment is not just a temporary break in communication; it often lasts for extended periods, ranging from hours to days or even weeks. During this time, the abuser may completely shut down and refuse to engage in any meaningful conversation.

- Manipulative Intent - The abuser uses silence as a means of punishment or control, aiming to make you feel guilty, anxious, or desperate for their attention. They may use the silent treatment as a way to assert dominance and gain power in the relationship.

- Emotional Impact - The 'Silent Knight' abuse tactic can have a profound emotional impact on you and any children you have together. The abuser's lack of their consistent presence can allow you and your children to feel rejected, confused, and insignificant. You may find yourself working tirelessly to explain yourself or trying to prove that you are worthy of their love, time, and affection.

- Communication Breakdown - 'Silent Knight' erodes open and healthy communication in the relationship. The lack of dialogue prevents conflict resolution, addressing concerns, and building emotional intimacy, leading to a breakdown in trust and connection.

If any of these signs look familiar to you, I want to challenge you to talk to someone about it - today. Co-parenting or dealing with an abuser who uses this abuse tactic can be challenging when you navigate it alone. If you have not experienced this, I want you to share something on your social media educating your followers about the topics.

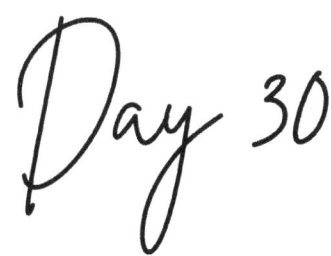

Day 30

Yesterday, we talked about the 'Silent Knight' and what it looks like as an abuse tactic. Today, I want you to reflect on your experience with it.

Have you ever experienced this form of abuse before? If so, how do you feel it impacted you? If you haven't, what would you say to someone experiencing it now?

I am a survivor.
My strength has
no limits.

MY SELF LOVE GROWS STRONGER EACH AND EVERY DAY

I deserve safe love.

The Doctor's Orders

Over the last several weeks, we have covered a ton of information. Hopefully, you now feel more confident having discussions on domestic violence and the many different ways in which it can occur.

As we step into this next month, I want to challenge you. I want to encourage you to go deeper during these times of reflection. In fact, don't be ashamed to staple a few more pages if you find that I didn't leave you enough space to write it all out. Remember, this is meant to be your safe space to heal. You can only do that when you reveal those inner thoughts that keep tormenting you through this process.

Before we continue with our next daily activity, I want you to stop and reflect. Using all of the information and tactics that you've learned about so far, I want you to complete the next exercise titled: Have I Been Abused? I want you to be as detailed as possible as you fill out each section.

Once you are finished with this next exercies, I want you to jump into the journal prompt for today.

Keep going warrior. You've got this.

Dr. Allanah Roberts-Headley

HAVE I BEEN ABUSED?

Now, we are going to spend some time focusing on ways that you may have experienced abuse.

Using the definitions from the last section, we are going to dive deep into each one. I encourage you to challenge yourself here. You can't heal what you won't reveal. **If you keep lying to yourself, the only person you are hurting is you.**

Don't be afraid of the emotions that may come up as you complete some of these tasks. Anger is normal. You may feel irritated and disappointed all at the exact same time. That's OK, too. **There is no right way to heal.** There is no finish line for you to aspire for. This will be a day-to-day, minute-to-minute, second-to-second, kind of life for a while. Just do the best that you can do right now. Push yourself, and then follow through. You've got this.

Which types of abuse have you experienced?

Did you know all of these versions of abuse existed? If not, which one surprised you the most?

Which types of abuse do you want more information on? Why?

Did you see any of these types of abuse tactics used when you were a child? If you answer yes to this question, please use the space below to get some of that weight you've been carrying off. Share as much as you want about the experiences that you have lived through.

Domestic Violence is a scary thing to a child and can have lasting impacts on the way they view themselves and the world around them. Using your own life experiences, how do you think a child is impacted by domestic violence?

If you experienced domestic violence as a child, can you see any similarities or patterns between your life as a child and the lives of your children?

As we wrap up this exercise, I want to leave you with this very important truth. You are not your circumstances or present situation. You can only be held to the standard of what you know. If, prior to this exercise, you didn't realize you were experiencing a form of abuse, don't be so hard on yourself. However, now that you know better - we have to do better. Why? Because only fools receive knowledge and don't use it.

Now, I want to challenge you to use the space below to write out a simple promise for the rest of the week. It doesn't need to be anything long or wordy. It can be as simple as not setting a second snooze alarm or deciding to drink at least eight glasses of water throughout the day. Then, write out some things you can do to help you achieve your goal.

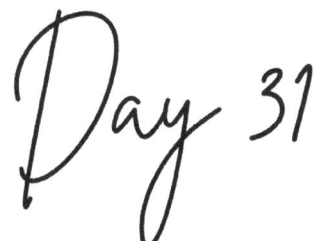

Day 31

Today, I want you to choose from one of the journal prompts below and write on it. If you really want to challenge yourself, answer them both.

1. What would I say if I were to write a letter to my body about how I've allowed it to be treated?

2. What is my biggest fear about this new chapter?

Day 32

The **cycle of abuse** is addicting because it is usually done in a pattern. Our body eventually gets used to the "safety" of knowing what is coming next. As anyone addicted to something, our minds convince us that we *need* this thing to survive.

Today, I want to talk about the different stages of the cycle of abuse. While I'm not leaving you any assignments to write out today, my hope is that you will study this cycle until you memorize it.

Knowing is always half the battle. Once you have a full understanding of each cycle, you can quickly identify that stage in the future. This will give you the courage and power that you need to disrupt those patterns if you ever see them happening again.

How Could This Happen to You?

Believe it or not, that dreadful question is going to come up often. For those who have never experienced domestic violence or any of the ways that it shows up, it is a genuine question. Let's talk about that for a minute.

No one ever willingly signs up to be manipulated, used, and abused. No. Abusers know that, and for this reason, they use a set of tactics that invokes the **cycle of abuse.** This cycle includes four separate stages.

The Four Stages of the Abuse Cycle

1. Tension Building Phase
2. Explosive Phase
3. Honeymoon Phase
4. Calm Phase

In the beginning, abusers may get victims accustomed to this cycle by violating small boundaries. They may push your buttons by making light of something private that you've shared with them. They may even make an inappropriate comment about your friend or family member. All of this is a ploy to see how far past the boundary line they can get. This is where the cycle of abuse begins. The moment that someone has willingly made the decision to violate a clear boundary of yours, it's obvious. They plan to use and abuse your love. They will forever find new ways to cross every boundary you are forced to create just to survive.

Once this person violates you the first time, you are often left feeling very confused. You don't know what to believe. Some of us grew up in an environment where domestic violence was rampant, so that behavior was expected. For others, your entrapment in the abuse cycle is usually only noticeable once it has grown too big to hide. Because you may not have been taught to have or recognize healthy coping skills, you may easily find yourself in the **tension-building phase**. During this part of the cycle of abuse, you may even *feel* the tension growing between you and your partner, and before you know it, you will be walking on eggshells, trying to avoid upsetting them further. You will find that they will be easily angered or frustrated, and you may find yourself doing anything to get them to return to a version you are used to dealing with.

Then it happens. During the **explosive phase**, the tension has officially reached its peak. The first time you encounter this in your relationship, it may not originally start off with violence. Instead, your partner may use abusive language they have never used with you before. Your partner may snatch something out of your hand, drive recklessly, or break something precious to you during their outburst.

The next phase you will experience will be the **honeymoon phase**. During this part of the abuse cycle, your abuser will go back to the person you know and love. In fact, they may even go above and beyond their usual behaviors. This is done to get you to forget about what just happened. In fact, they may use gracious gifts and apologies as an excuse not to "focus on the past." Their goal during this part of the cycle of abuse is to distract you from the abusive behavior you just encountered.

Because that first encounter with abuse in a relationship is not always something that is easy to identify or explain to others, we tend to give our partners the benefit of the doubt. We accept their love-bombing behaviors during the honeymoon phase and casually stroll into the **calm phase** of the cycle of abuse. During this part of the cycle, your relationship has gone back to "normal." You now have the confidence that this was just a one-off situation and your partner will never do that again. This stage is the one that holds a lot of us captive. Because we have ignored our own needs and accepted the behavior that was hard to process, we have essentially joined in on the programming that allows us to get used to this cycle.

This is how people find themselves trapped in abusive relationships. Notice how that first cycle isn't always something drastic, so it is possible that someone who is not familiar with the cycles of abuse will continue to do this song and dance with someone until it gets worse. I say that with confidence because it is true. Once someone realizes that they have power and control over you, it is not going to go away. In fact, it has the potential to progressively get worse as our inability to leave teaches them that we are somehow okay with their behavior.

Please understand that the length and intensity of each phase can vary from one abusive relationship to another. Some cycles may occur over days, while others may span weeks or months. You may find yourself trapped in this cycle, desperately clinging to the moments of calm and love during the honeymoon phase, hoping that change is possible.

I am here to tell you that change is definitely going to happen if you continue to stay in that relationship or go back to it. I can guarantee you that what will change will be you.

Over time, you will lose the parts of yourself that you once adored and admired. You will begin to see yourself in the same light that your abuser sees you. You will change your friend groups as you now have to hide the abuse from the ones that you love. You will change how you dress, walk, and talk as their ever-changing needs keep you tip-toeing on eggshells. Yes. Change is going to come, but is it worth it when you count up what you will lose in order to keep that abusive partner?

Keaidy's Two Cents

From my experience, this is how it started. Then, over time, the cycle may skip a step or two. In a worst-case scenario, the times of peace get longer, and the explosions are more intense. Either way, being empowered to identify each phase is going to be key in your healing journey.

The cycle of abuse can be a challenging one to disrupt by yourself. I highly encourage you to work with either your therapist or a local domestic violence agency as you move through this season. Processing your grief while trying to disrupt patterns and creating new ones is a lot to handle. It's okay to let others know you need more assistance in this season.

Essence of Survival

I know that you didn't plan to end up in this situation. In fact, I'm confident that you, like a lot of other survivors, were shocked the day that you finally accepted that you were in an abusive relationship. That's because the cycle of abuse doesn't always start off wild and drastic. Abusers may often take you through this cycle several times using other forms of abuse before ever getting physical. Some relationships may never get there, but increase in intensity. Noticing this cycle and the different phases is what is going to help you as you move forward with your life. I need you to know this cycle because when you can easily identify it, you have the power and control to disrupt it.

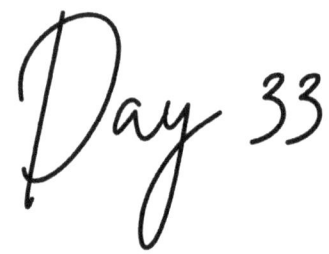

Day 33

Yesterday, we learned all about the abuse cycle. We talked about the **tension-building phase, the explosive phase, the honeymoon phase, and the calm phase**. Today, I want you to explain each phase in your own words. Then, on the following page, I want you to write a letter to yourself. In that letter, I need you to show yourself some grace as you expose the times you missed each cycle in the past.

a letter to myself...

Day 34

Today, I want you to choose from one of the journal prompts below and write on it. If you really want to challenge yourself, answer them both.

1. How did your abuser manipulate or control you psychologically, and how did that make you feel?

2. How has physical abuse impacted your relationships with your friends and family?

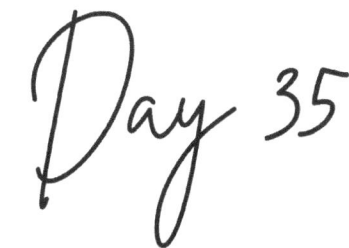

Characteristics of Abusers

Not all abusers share the same characteristics; however, they all have the same goals in mind. **Abusers want power and control over you.** Today, let's take a minute to talk about some of the characteristics that we may find in an abuser.

- **Abusers display controlling behavior:** Remember, their long-term goal is to control every aspect of your life. They control who you see, talk to and what you can do with your time. In the early stages of the relationship, they will often times mask their concern for your safety and well-being. They can ask for you to share your location, provide them with passwords to your phone or social media accounts, and may even 'joke' about putting a tracker on your car. The point of these tactics is to keep a tight leash on you so they are able to force you into isolation, where they can limit your access to anyone but them.

- **Abusers are often very jealous and possessive:** Some abusers will accuse you of cheating even though they don't have evidence or proof. This tactic is to get you to expose yourself to them. Oftentimes, we may volunteer passwords or give up some of our privacy in an effort to make the abuser feel more at ease.

- **Abusers are manipulative:** A powerful tactic for an abuser is to manipulate you and the way that you see them and the world around you. To do this, they will manipulate you. They may call you names, belittle, and humiliate you. They may also use tactics like gaslighting and brainwashing to convince you that you are the sole problem in the relationship. They may also use these tactics to convince you that you cannot trust any of your family or friends. This is done so that you only rely on your abuser.

- **Abusers rarely take accountability or responsibility:** Abusers will shift the blame in an effort to avoid responsibility. They may try to manipulate you into believing that you are the reason that they responded the way that they did. They may even make excuses or find ways to minimize the abuse that you have experienced

- **Abusers may use threats and intimidations:** Remember, not all abuse is physical. Some abusers will threaten violence against you, themselves, or those that you love. This is done to intimidate you so they can reinforce the power

- (continued) and control they believe they have over you.
- **Explosive Anger:** Abusers oftentimes struggle to manage their own emotions. This can be seen with wild outbursts of anger - even over minor issues. This anger can then escalate to verbal or physical abuse.
- **Abusers try to keep you isolated:** Abusers will isolate you from family or friends because it is easier to control and manipulate you if they have you all to themselves.
- **Abusers will use the cycles of abuse for their benefit:** Abusers can often be predictable as they follow the cycle of abuse. Remember, they may take you through that cycle several times before getting physical. The point is to get you comfortable and addicted to the cycle. Because our brains naturally love patterns, we eventually feel 'safe' in this pattern.
- **Abusers may find ways to control your finances:** Abusers may withhold money, monitor your spending, or prevent you from working. This is all done to keep you fully dependent on them.
- **Abusers may use the Silent Knight:** Abusers may refuse to engage with you unless you act the way that they want you to. They can withhold love, attention, time with your children, and affection until you are willing to do things their way.
- **Abusers may force you to do things you are uncomfortable with**: In a healthy relationship, you should be able to tell your partner no. However, because abusers want to control you, they will never accept a no from you. In fact, they may even force you to do things you would never do under normal circumstances. They may force you to give them money, have sex with others, do drugs, or drink. All of these things will later be used against you, but for now, they force you to do it in order to show the control they feel they have over you.
- **Abusers may follow strict gender roles:** Sometimes, abusers will adhere to strict gender roles. This means they can expect you to do things you feel are oppressive and restricting.

Essence of Survival

Recognizing the characteristics of an abuser is imperative if you want to avoid running into another one in the future. Today, I want you to take a moment to reflect on the signs that you missed. Using the space on the next page, I want you to write down all of the ways that your previous abuser(s) showed red flags in the beginning. Take a moment to consider why you didn't recognize them as red flags, and write out how you plan to handle the situation the next time you are ever presented with someone who displays some of these red flags.

Day 36

Today, I want you to choose from one of the journal prompts below and write on it. If you really want to challenge yourself, answer them both.

1. Reflect on the progress you've made on your healing journey. What traits have you learned about yourself through this process?
2. How has your perspective on healthy relationships evolved since the abuse?

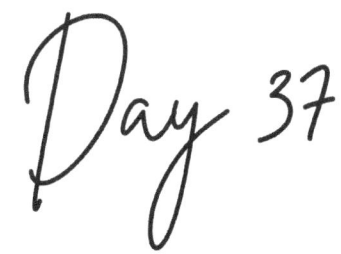

Case Study #1

To better understand the cycles of abuse, I wanted to give you a few examples of how it can look. Read the following case study and then answer the questions that follow.

Newton and Katie were in a relationship that seemed promising at first. Newton appeared caring and attentive, and Katie felt lucky to have found someone who made her feel special. However, over time, things started to change after they had a child together.

Tension-Building Phase
The relationship began to experience increasing tension. As Katie began to lose the baby weight she gained from her recent pregnancy, Newton became increasingly jealous and possessive. Katie felt like she was constantly walking on eggshells, trying not to set him off. She noticed his temper was becoming more unpredictable, and the fear of triggering his anger loomed over her.

Explosive Phase
Eventually, the tension reached its breaking point. Newton's anger would explode into verbal attacks, berating Katie with hurtful words that would chip away at her self-esteem. Sometimes, the abuse turned physical. Newton would sit on Katie in an effort to keep her from leaving whenever she got tired of his abuse. These explosive episodes left her emotionally shattered, unable to understand why someone who claimed to love her could treat her this way.

Honeymoon Phase
Following the explosive episodes, Newton would often show remorse and apologize profusely. He would shower Katie with affection, gifts, and promises of change. During these moments, Katie allowed herself to hope that things would improve. She believed Newton's apologies and longed for the loving partner she thought she

had initially met.

Calm Phase

In the calm phase, the relationship would return to "normal." Newton's behavior would appear normal, and Katie would convince herself that the worst was behind them. She desperately clung to these peaceful moments, yearning for a stable and loving relationship.

However, the cycle would repeat itself. The tension would slowly build up again, leading to another explosive episode, followed by the honeymoon phase and a brief period of calm. This repetitive cycle of abuse left Katie feeling trapped, confused, and emotionally drained.

Please note: The cycle of abuse is not limited to any specific timeline. It can vary in duration and intensity from one relationship to another. Recognizing the pattern of abuse is essential for survivors like Katie to understand that they are not to blame for the abuse inflicted upon them. It helps them realize that the abuser's actions are a choice driven by a need for power and control.

Now, take a minute to answer these three questions:

1. How did Newton's behavior align with the tension-building phase of the abuse cycle?
2. Describe the explosive phase in the context of Newton and Katie's relationship.
3. Why do you think Katie found it difficult to leave the relationship, even during the calm phase?

Day 38

Today, I want you to choose from one of the journal prompts below and write on it. If you really want to challenge yourself, answer them both.

1. Take a moment to write out your scariest moment of physical abuse. How did that incident change you?
2. How has your experience with abuse changed your perception of love?

I AM IN CONTROL OF MY THOUGHTS, EMOTIONS, AND ACTIONS

I am enough.

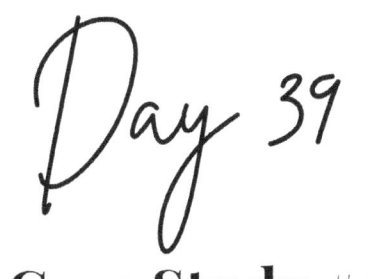

Day 39

Case Study #2

Let's explore another case study together.

Julie found herself trapped in a terrifying and abusive relationship with Jason. Jason's drinking habit had escalated over time, leading to frequent episodes of physical violence. Julie was not only subjected to the brunt of his anger, but also faced the agonizing fear for the safety of her two children from a previous relationship.

Tension-Building Phase
The relationship was always rocky. Jason's mood would become increasingly volatile, especially when he had been drinking. Julie tried to anticipate his every need because she was trying to avoid triggering his rage. The fear of setting him off and the constant tension took a toll on her mental and emotional well-being.

Explosive Phase
As the tension reached its peak, Jason's anger would erupt in violent outbursts. He would physically assault Julie, leaving her with bruises, cuts, and lasting emotional scars. He would also threaten to harm her children if she disclosed the abuse to anyone, instilling a deep sense of terror in Julie. She felt trapped and helpless, fearing for the safety of her family.

Honeymoon Phase
Following each abusive episode, Jason would enter the honeymoon phase. He would shower Julie with attention. He would make her breakfast in bed, make a sweet post about her on social media, and promise that he was going to change. During these periods, Julie held onto hope that Jason would truly transform and that their relationship could be salvaged. She yearned for the loving partner she had once believed Jason to be.

Calm Phase

In the calm phase, the relationship would briefly stabilize. Jason's behavior would return to a seemingly normal state, creating an illusion of peace and security. Julie longed for this tranquility and desperately wanted to believe that things would remain peaceful.

However, the cycle of abuse would inevitably repeat itself. The tension would build again, leading to another explosive episode, followed by the honeymoon phase and a temporary period of calm. This repetitive pattern of abuse left Julie feeling hopeless and constantly exhausted.

Now, take a minute to answer these three questions:
- How did Jason's behavior align with the tension-building phase of the abuse cycle?
- Describe the explosive phase in the context of Jason and Julie's relationship.
- Why do you think Julie found it hard to disclose the abuse and seek help, given the threats Jason made against her children?

Day 40

Today, I want you to choose from one of the journal prompts below and write on it. If you really want to challenge yourself, answer them both.

1. Describe the ways you've learned to prioritize your safety and well-being since leaving the abuser.
2. How do you plan to stay safe in future relationships?

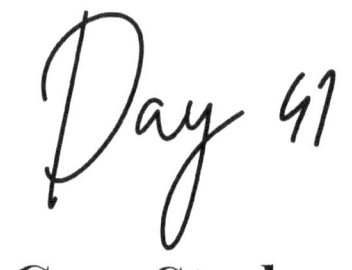

Case Study #3

Ashley, a devout Catholic, found herself entangled in a toxic relationship with Andrew. Initially, she was drawn to him because they shared the same faith and beliefs. Andrew convinced Ashley they were destined to be together, claiming that God had ordained their union. Despite having a baby out of wedlock, Ashley held onto the hope that their relationship would eventually align with their religious values.

Tension-Building Phase

The relationship was marked by escalating tension. Andrew would use his religious beliefs as a means of control, interpreting the Bible to justify his actions. Ashley felt pressured to conform to his expectations, fearing that straying from his interpretation would be a sin. As the tension mounted, Ashley found herself suppressing her needs and desires to appease Andrew's religious demands.

Explosive Phase

In the explosive phase, Andrew's infidelity became evident. Despite claiming to follow their shared religious principles, he engaged in unprotected sexual relationships with other women. He manipulated Ashley, using the guise of their faith to justify his actions, suggesting that divorce was not an option in the eyes of God. Ashley was left devastated, struggling to reconcile her religious beliefs with the betrayal and mistreatment she endured.

Honeymoon Phase

Following each episode of infidelity, Andrew would enter the honeymoon phase. He would shower Ashley with apologies, profess his love, and promise to change his ways. During these periods, Ashley clung to the hope that Andrew's words were sincere, desperately seeking reconciliation and a return to the harmony they once shared.

Calm Phase

In the calm phase, the relationship would temporarily stabilize. Andrew would create an illusion of religious devotion, appearing committed to rebuilding trust and honoring their vows. Ashley yearned for this stability, longing for the sanctity of their union as dictated by their faith.

However, the cycle of abuse would inevitably repeat itself. The tension would build again, leading to another explosive episode, followed by the honeymoon phase and a temporary period of calm. This repetitive pattern of abuse left Ashley feeling hopeless and constantly exhausted.

Now, take a minute to answer these three questions:
- How did Andrew's behavior align with the tension-building phase of the abuse cycle?
- Describe the explosive phase in the context of Andrew and Ashley's relationship.
- Why do you think Ashley found it hard to leave Jason despite his infidelity and abusive ways?

The Doctor's Orders

In the depths of healing and self-discovery, it is crucial to embrace and honor the vessel that carries us through life: our body. As survivors of domestic violence, we have endured unimaginable challenges and trauma, often leaving us disconnected from our physical selves. But over the next few days, I want you to explore some serious topics with me. We're going on a journey of reclaiming our bodies and rediscovering the love and appreciation that they deserve.

Loving our bodies may seem like an uphill battle when we've been conditioned to believe that our worth is defined by other people, distorted by the abuse we have been through. Yet, as we delve into loving our bodies and ourselves, we will gradually uncover a profound truth: our bodies are not to blame for the abuse inflicted upon us. Our bodies, in all their resilience, strength, and vulnerability, should be celebrated and cherished.

In these pages, we will unravel the complicated connection between abuse, trauma, and our physical and mental well-being. We will shed light on the cycles of abuse, recognizing that they are not an outcome of our actions or shortcomings. Instead, they are the result of deliberate choices made by those seeking to maintain power and control. By understanding this truth, we can free ourselves from the burden of self-blame and embark on a path of self-love and healing.

As we explore the impact of trauma on our bodies and minds, we will encounter the common responses that arise from surviving such experiences. We will learn that our reactions, both physical and mental, are not signs of weakness, but manifestations of the strength and resilience that reside within us. Through this understanding, we can cultivate compassion and acceptance for ourselves, realizing that we are survivors with immeasurable courage.

I pray these pages are a source of inspiration and empowerment, reminding us all that our bodies have carried us through the darkest moments, and now have the potential to lead us toward a future filled with self-discovery, healing, and self-love.

Dr. Allanah Roberts-Headley

Day 42

Trauma & Your Body

Through trauma, our bodies bear the scars of the past. Over the next few days, we are going to explore the physical and mental effects of abuse, highlighting the importance of self-love and appreciation. Our bodies, although they are resilient and remarkable, deserve compassion. Today, I want you to write an apology letter to your body. How do you plan to treat yourself better moving forward?

Today, I want to challenge you to incorporate something that helps you connect with your body. Guided meditation is a great practice that can help you. If that is something you already practice, try going for a walk today or incorporating a form of exercise that your doctor has approved. Then, use the space below to journal about your experience.

Day 43

Physical Effects of Trauma

Hyper-vigilance and Startle Responses

Some survivors who have experienced trauma may develop a heightened sense of alertness and hypervigilance. They may constantly scan their environment for potential threats, leading to increased startle responses, heart palpitations, and an overall sense of being on edge.

Chronic Pain and Tension

Traumatic experiences can manifest in physical symptoms such as chronic pain, tension headaches, migraines, and muscle stiffness. The body may hold onto stress and tension, resulting in physical discomfort and reduced well-being.

Immune System Dysregulation

Trauma can impact the immune system, making individuals more susceptible to illnesses and infections. Chronic stress and trauma can weaken the immune response, leaving survivors more vulnerable to physical ailments and longer recovery times.

Sleep Disturbances

Trauma can disrupt normal sleep patterns, leading to difficulties falling asleep, staying asleep, or experiencing restful sleep. Survivors may suffer from insomnia, nightmares, or night sweats, which can further contribute to fatigue and a compromised immune system.

Chronic Fatigue

Trauma-related stress can result in persistent fatigue, exhaustion, and a feeling of being physically drained, even after adequate rest.

Neurological Symptoms

Trauma can affect the functioning of the nervous system, leading to neurological symptoms such as headaches, migraines, dizziness, memory problems, and difficulty concentrating.

Changes in Eating Patterns

Trauma can disrupt eating patterns, leading to changes in appetite, overeating, undereating, or developing disordered eating behaviors such as binge eating or restrictive eating.

Cardiovascular Effects

Trauma can contribute to cardiovascular issues, including high blood pressure, heart palpitations, and an increased risk of heart disease.

Gastrointestinal Issues

Trauma can impact the digestive system, leading to gastrointestinal problems such as stomachaches, irritable bowel syndrome (IBS), nausea, and digestive disturbances. The gut-brain connection plays a significant role, and trauma-related stress can disrupt the functioning of the digestive system.

While I could go on explaining more ways that trauma effects your physical body, I hope you got the point. Using the space below, I want you to write out any physical symptoms you have dealt with.

Day 44

Reflection

Keaidy: I know firsthand just how challenging it can be to live your life as a survivor. In the beginning, your body may constantly be searching your surroundings for signs that you are safe. In fact, because you are now removed from the cycle of abuse that provided your brain with a sense of 'safety' from the pattern it provided, you may feel more uneasy out of your situation than you did in it.

Today, I want to invite you to take some time to talk about it. How do you feel now that you've had some time in your safe space? Has the transition been easy for you?

Day 45

Mental Effects of Trauma

Anxiety Disorders

Trauma survivors may develop various anxiety disorders, such as generalized anxiety disorder (GAD), panic disorder, or social anxiety disorder. These conditions can manifest as excessive worry, fear, panic attacks, and avoidance of triggering situations.

Disrupted Self-Image and Self-Esteem

Trauma can drastically change the value you have of yourself. Survivors may struggle with feelings of shame, guilt, and negative self-perception. You may also have difficulties trusting others or forming healthy relationships.

Emotional Dysregulation

Trauma can disrupt emotional regulation, leading to intense mood swings, anger outbursts, irritability, and difficulty managing emotions. You may also experience emotional numbing or dissociation as a coping mechanism to protect yourself from overwhelming feelings.

Depression

Trauma can increase your risk of developing depression. Survivors may experience persistent feelings of sadness, hopelessness, loss of interest in activities, changes in appetite or sleep patterns, and difficulties with concentration and decision-making.

Dissociation

Dissociation is a defense mechanism that the mind uses to cope with overwhelming trauma. It involves a disconnection from one's thoughts, feelings, memories, or even your own sense of identity.

Trust Issues

Trauma can erode your ability to trust others. You may struggle to form and maintain healthy relationships, often questioning others' motives or fearing vulnerability due to past betrayals.

Post-Traumatic Stress Disorder (PTSD)

PTSD is a common mental health condition that can develop following a traumatic event. Symptoms may include intrusive memories, flashbacks, nightmares, avoidance behaviors, hypervigilance, and emotional distress. PTSD can significantly impact daily functioning and quality of life.

Hyperarousal

Trauma can result in a heightened state of arousal and vigilance, making individuals more sensitive and reactive to potential threats. This can lead to increased irritability, difficulty concentrating, and an exaggerated startle response.

Guilt and Shame

Survivors of trauma often experience intense feelings of guilt and shame, blaming themselves for the traumatic event or the actions of the abuser. These feelings can be debilitating and impact one's self-esteem, self-worth, and ability to trust oneself.

In this box, I want you to list five coping/self-care techniques you've utilized or have learned in the past to help with any of the above-mentioned experiences.

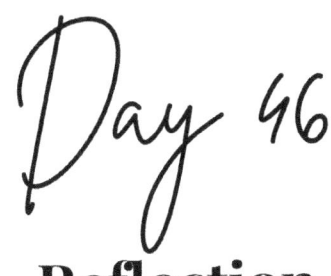

Reflection

Yesterday, we learned a lot about the mental effects that trauma has on your body. Today, I want to invite you to spend some time reflecting on what you learned and then identifying the ways that trauma has personally impacted you on your journey.

Take a moment to think about all of your experiences with abuse. How have those moments changed you from who you were before it started? Have your views on relationships changed since you now have experience with domestic violence? How has this altered how you see yourself?

Day 47

Today, I want you to choose from one of the journal prompts below and write on it. If you really want to challenge yourself, answer them both.

1. What emotions arise in you whenever you think about the past and the abuse that you have suffered?
2. What are some steps you can take to help you learn to trust others again?

Day 48

Today, I want you to have a moment to check your understanding of what you've learned over the last few days.

We spent some time talking about how trauma can impact your mental and physical well-being. That is why I want you to spend today putting what you've learned in your own words. Imagine someone you loved just admitted they are stuck in an abusive relationship. How would you warn them about the longstanding impacts of trauma?

Narcissistic Abuse

Earlier, we discussed various types of abuse and how they can manifest in different ways. I intentionally singled this one out for a reason.

Narcissistic abuse is a specific form of emotional and psychological abuse that is done by individuals who have been diagnosed with narcissistic personality disorder or by someone who displays narcissistic personality traits. These types of abusers are often talked about for their constant need for admiration, lack of empathy, and the overall sense of entitlement they live with.

The Most Skilled Manipulators

Narcissistic abusers are the most skilled manipulators you will ever meet. They will do whatever they need to in order to accomplish their desire to control your life. To their core, those with narcissistic personality disorder (or narcissistic personality traits) are incredibly insecure and fragile. This is why they often look for those with unhealed trauma. It is much easier to exploit you when they can easily identify the areas where you have been hurt.

The Familiarity of Dysfunction

Are you familiar with the expression that misery loves company? That is exactly what is happening in this kind of abusive relationship. Because narcissists do not love or appreciate themselves, they will do everything in their power to make sure that you one day have that same viewpoint about yourself. This is why they typically like victims who have previously suffered from some type of abuse.

Trauma Bonding

Some books make reference to Trauma Bonds as Stockholm syndrome, but these are fancy terms to explain that you have developed an emotional attachment or bond with your abuser. In psychology, there are seven steps in trauma bonding, and just like the abuse cycle, it is imperative to recognize each step if you ever plan on truly breaking free from the grip it holds on your life.

Stage One: Love Bombing

This is the 'honeymoon phase' where they shower you with love and affection. They may even give you gifts and a lot of emotional intimacy. Abusers use this period to manipulate you. It is important to realize that everything done in the love-bombing phase is all an act, as you will be spending the rest of your time trying to get them back to that version of themselves.

Also, during this time, these manipulators are using this time to gain very valuable insight into your deepest wants and desires. They may study you and seem to hang on to your every word as they are learning the best ways to manipulate you in the future.

Stage Two: Trust & Dependency

If you have lived your life feeling unloved, unseen, or rejected, the love-bombing phase of this kind of relationship can make you feel like you've hit the jackpot. That is why this next step is so easy for them to obtain.

Because they've learned all about your wants and desires, in this step, they are going to lay it on thick. They may agree to huge commitments to show you how much they care. They may start planning vacations or a future together. They do this so you will learn to not only trust them, but to depend on them also.

Stage Three: Criticism

Once they know they have you right where they want you, that is where you will experience their 'mask' coming off. It is during this phase that you will start to see the manipulator criticize everything you do or wear. They may state hurtful comments about your looks or call you nasty names.

Stage Four: Gaslighting and Manipulation

During this phase, the manipulator is going to do everything in their power to convince you that you are crazy. They do this in an effort to get you to question your own sanity. This happens when you call out your abuser for the hurtful things that they've said to you. Instead of taking accountability, in this phase, the abuser is going to shift the blame onto you. They may try to convince you that everything is your fault. They may try to convince you that you didn't see something that you know you did. At this time, they will stop at nothing to avoid taking any responsibility for their hurtful and abusive ways.

Stage Five: Resignation & Submission

By this time, a victim is so tired of the cycle that they will begin to compromise their core values and beliefs in an effort to avoid any more confrontation with the narcissist. This is where people-pleasing will come into play as the victim will give into the needs of the narcissist in order to avoid any more judgment or criticism.

Stage Six: Loss of Self

By this stage in the relationship, a victim has submitted so much of who they are that most don't recognize themselves anymore. Some of my clients have described this as feeling like a shell of their former selves. It is during this time that a victim may realize how much they have given up in order to maintain that abusive relationship. The isolation and realization of their reality can be incredibly difficult to deal with. That is why a lot of clients will report feeling suicidal during this phase. It is hard for them to like the person they see in the mirror, and they feel so far removed from the person they were before the abuse.

Stage Seven: Addiction to the Cycle

Didn't we recently study another cyclical pattern that has a tendency to become addictive? This one is no different. As I stated earlier in this journey, our brains love patterns. In fact, it gives us a false sense of safety when the brain feels like it knows what to expect next. While it cannot predict what the abuser is going to say or do next, the brain does realize what step goes next in the cyclical pattern. For this reason, we become addicted.

Essence of Survival

Breaking out of this cycle can be a hard and devastating thing to do. After all, our bodies are usually addicted to this process by the time we realize we mentally cannot handle it anymore.

Narcissistic abuse can be a lot to unpack because of how twisted the psychological abuse can get. Tomorrow, we will unpack some of the characteristics, but for today, I want you to study the seven stages of trauma bonding.

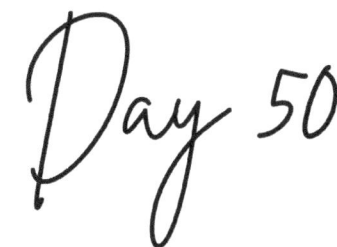

Narcissistic Characteristics

Yesterday, we spent a lot of time talking about narcissistic abuse and the seven stages of trauma bonding. Today, I want to shed light on some of the characteristics. Below are some common narcissistic characteristics and behaviors.

- **Grandiosity:** Narcissists have a huge ego to make up for their low self-esteem. They try to convince everyone that they are special or unique. They will also exaggerate their gifts, talents, and achievements.
- **Need for Attention and Validation:** Narcissists crave admiration from others. They are constantly in need of a "supply" that can make them feel better about themselves.
- **Sense of Entitlement:** Narcissists believe that the rules never apply to them. They expect special treatment and privileges.
- **Lack of Empathy:** Narcissists struggle to care about the needs of other people.
- **Manipulation:** Narcissists are skilled manipulators. In fact, if you continue your studies on narcissistic personality disorder, you'll find several different types of narcissists. This is because they don't all use the same tactics or strategies.
- **Superficial Relationships:** Everything around the narcissist is to fuel their need to be grand and important. This is why they engage in a lot of superficial and transactional relationships. Thanks to their lack of empathy for others, they lack some of the skills necessary to build lasting bonds.
- **Arrogance:** Narcissists like to appear like they are better than everyone else. This will be displayed through their arrogance.
- **Impulsivity:** Some narcissists show impulsive behaviors. Oftentimes, they do things to get what they want, so they don't always take the time to slow down and consider the consequences.

Again, this doesn't include all of the intricacies of being in a relationship with someone who suffers from narcissistic personality disorder; however, I wanted to make sure that I spent some time discussing it as it often comes up in my line of work. Tomorrow, we are going to learn about common characteristics that narcissists look for when they are seeking out their new supply, and that is the biggest gem I truly want you to take away from all of this.

Essence of Survival

Have you been in a relationship with someone who was diagnosed with NPD? Have you dated someone who displayed a lot of these characteristics? If so, I want you to use the box below to journal your experience. If you have not been in a relationship with someone like that, how would you protect yourself if you come across someone with NPD behaviors?

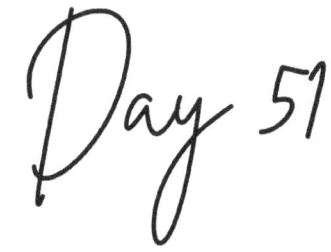

What Narcissistic Abusers Look For

These types of manipulators seek out partners whom they believe they can easily exploit. Oftentimes, they like victims who possess certain characteristics. While every abuser's preference is different, here are some common traits narcissistic abusers look for.

- **Empathetic & Nurturing:** Narcissistic abusers are drawn to people who are empathetic and caring. This is because they believe it is usually easier for them to take advantage of your kindness.
- **Low Self-Esteem:** People with low self-esteem will typically take more of the narcissist's treatment because they may not believe they deserve more than what they are receiving. This is why it is imperative that we heal after traumatic experiences. If we do not, we leave ourselves wide open for another manipulator to use to their advantage.
- **Dependent:** Narcissists often target those they feel will eventually become dependent on them. They seek out those who may need them financially or emotionally because it is easier to keep a victim trapped when they are reliant on their abuser.
- **People-Pleasers:** People who have a strong desire to please others and avoid conflict are typically more willing to accept abusive behavior.
- **Isolated:** Narcissists love those who prefer to self-isolate because it means that they won't have to do it for you.
- **High Tolerance for Emotional Pain:** This is why I am a big advocate of making others earn the right to hear your story. When we share our past experiences, narcissists will assume that because you've been through it in the past, you have a high tolerance to put up with whatever they put you through.
- **Lack of Boundaries:** Narcissists love those who have a difficult time setting, enforcing, and honoring their boundaries because they plan on doing whatever they want anyway.
- **Unrealistic Beliefs in Change:** Sometimes victims will have this belief that they may be able to love someone past their pain or that they can 'fix' their partner.

- (continued) Narcissists will exploit this by promising to change and improve the relationship.
- **Successful:** The better you appear to the public, the better you look for their image. That is why some narcissists love powerful people. If you are in a position of power or influence, narcissistic abusers may try to trap you into a relationship with them so they can use your status to look more important.

Essence of Survival

Today, we learned a lot about the characteristics that make a victim susceptible to this kind of abuse. In the box below, I want you to list out (using the list above) what traits you identify with. Then, I want you to consider some boundaries that you can put in place to help protect yourself.

Day 52

What are three things that you are thankful for today? It doesn't matter how big or how small. Take a moment to rest in the gratitude you have.

Day 53

Today, I want you to have a moment to check your understanding of what you've learned over the last few days.

We spent some time talking about NPD, trauma bonds, and the characteristics that narcissistic abusers look for when they are seeking out their next victim. With all of the information that you have learned, I want you to explain what you've just learned to someone else. Use the space below to explain what you have learned in your own words.

Day 54

Today, I want you to choose from one of the journal prompts below and write on it. If you really want to challenge yourself, answer them both.

1. Write about when you allowed yourself to grieve the losses you experienced due to the abuse.
2. How can you contribute to strengthening your safety plan and feeling more secure?

Day 55

Today, I want you to choose from one of the journal prompts below and write on it. If you really want to challenge yourself, answer them both.

1. What is something that you wish more people understood about domestic violence? How can you help spread the word?
2. Reflect on the time that you told someone about the abuse. How did it make you feel?

Day 56

Today, I want you to write a letter to your future self. Using the space below, I want you to write an intimate letter to the version of yourself that you one day want to show up as in the world.

a letter to my future self...

Day 57

Today, I want you to choose from one of the journal prompts below and write on it. If you really want to challenge yourself, answer them both.

1. Describe the first step you took toward seeking help or a safer life.
2. Take a moment to reflect on some of the red flags that you missed in the past. How do you plan to avoid this in the future?

Day 58

Keaidy: Throughout my healing journey, I've put in effort to shape a vision for every part of my life. I did this for my business, my home, and even my future partner. Over time, I've learned that it is easy to get distracted and thrown off course with temporary moments of lust. Take a moment to envision your next relationship and write it down below. I've left a personal example for you below.

My Vision of Love..

I leave myself open to get a new vision for love life and future partner.

Day 59

Today, I want you to choose from one of the journal prompts below and write on it. If you really want to challenge yourself, answer them both.

1. Have you had any recurring nightmares since leaving your abuser? If so, write them out below.

2. Have you ever blamed yourself for the abuse? Why or why not?

Day 60

Today, I want you to write out ten things that you wish you knew about abuse sooner. Then, I challenge you to share at least one of those things with someone you love.

_____

1.

2.

3.

4.

5.

6.

7.

8.

9.

10.

The Doctor's Orders

For the last 60 days, you've remained faithful to the decision that you made for yourself. I am so proud of you.

In these last thirty days, I plan on giving you only one journal prompt each day. This is to get you to dig a little deeper than you have up until this point. I will also include some activities that require you to do work outside of this workbook. This is only to help you develop habits that will keep you focused as you move on to doing your healing work without me.

Keep up the good work. You've got this.

Dr. Allanah Roberts-Headley

Day 61

Today, I want you to take a moment to reflect on the last sixty days. Can you think of five things you are grateful for? Can you think of five positive changes that you've made in your life? Once you've figured out your list, write them below.

Day 62

Oftentimes, a lot of us choose our abusers because something about the chaos they bring reminds us of "home."

Knowing this information, I want you to spend some time reflecting on the early lessons you learned about love. Take a moment to reflect on what you saw and heard growing up and then spend some time comparing and contrasting your relationship against those lessons.

Day 63

Self-Care Should Be a Priority

Keaidy: Self-care is a foundational piece of self-love. This is because we cannot pour from an empty cup.

Oftentimes, when we leave these abusive situations, we are riddled with anxiety and a to-do list that is a mile long. A lot of survivors may even have additional requirements if the Department of Children and Families was brought in as a result of the abuse. It is for this reason that I need you to start prioritizing yourself.

You cannot pour from an empty cup, and that is why you must prioritize things in the day that will fill you back up.

Poetry is one of those things for me. Poetry allows me the chance to be free and completely myself. I don't care about other people's thoughts and opinions; I just write down the things that flow naturally to me.

I'm going to share a poem with you, and then I want you to share something similar with me. Take a moment to write a line or two and share it on social media. Let us celebrate you by adding #EssenceofSurvival to your post.

Pretty Prison
by: Keaidy Bennett (Survivor)

Isolated
And all alone
In this place that you call my home.
I guess that's every good warden's job.
You know, to act like this treatment is some kind of favor.
Just to tell me that if I take it without any fight, I'll be rewarded for good behavior
In reality, we both know the truth.
It's crazy because out there

Somewhere
Is a poor fool praying for what I wish I could escape:
A home with a man to help her inhabit it.
She's blinded by the promises that she can't see the grit
And grime
That comes from sharing a space with a man who sometimes makes her feel like just
existing is a crime.
If only she could see beyond the beautiful brick walls
And really dwell inside
Not to be hypnotized
By the bay windows and crown molding
So she can really see what these four walls are holding –
Prisoners.

We're just prisoners of his pretty prison,
So, of course, we have to be
Isolated
And all alone
In this "home,"
So no one can hear our screams
Or our cries
Or the lies he tells himself that he's really a good guy
When in reality, we all know the truth.
Hurt people hurt people
Because it's hard for them to escape that painful prison of their mind
That seems to run on the pain that it was once fed at some time.
Left to feel
Isolated
And all alone
In the memories of the things they can't forget,
So they continue the cycle as if the position they now play gives them power over it.
In reality,
It just shows exactly how weak and wounded they are
Sharing scars

And throwing hurtful words around like dangerous explosives
Because they can't stand up – face the mirror – and just forgive who really hurt them.
They've taken their internalized nightmares just to make it a reality for some unsuspecting victim.
Their mental prison
Now has a legitimate address.
And no matter how much it costs to run
Or how decorative it is,
It still is what it is –
A pretty prison.
Just a place where these four walls
Can make acres feel small
Since they'll close right in
All because he doesn't know how to handle his emotions.
It's like he missed the memo that even though we show it differently, we are all battling and dealing with something.
I wish I could tell him,
"Being stressed shouldn't justify you to use those hands I thought would protect me as weapons.
And being angry isn't an excuse to use that tongue that once spit game
And caused certain lady parts to go insane
To spew out such words of hate.

Life would seem worth it
Once you realize that everyone isn't perfect
And forgive who you're really mad at
Because in case your wounded ego has you too blind to see,
I am not them.
All I've tried to do was be your friend
And lover until the end
And sadly, I feel like we've finally gotten there.
You see, I no longer feel welcomed here.
Your pretty prison seems overcrowded by your fears, insecurities, and the crap that you just won't let go of.

Although love never dies,
It can be killed,
And regardless of my past mistakes
I don't deserve to be in such a maximum-security prison with a criminal who thinks
it's okay to murder spirits and assassinate someone else's character.
I really tried to hold on to love you past your pain cause I've been there before,
But I can't do anything more to help you when that wall you've built to protect
yourself does its job from preventing others from really ever getting in.

And although someone who looks like you
In a home that looks something like this
Is how I always imagined it,
I just can't do it anymore.
Because life,
No matter how pretty the picture is,
Just doesn't seem worth it
When all I want to do is love without limits and be free and happy to dance
But instead,
With your presence,
I'm forced to only tip-toe on eggshells.

Using the space provided. I want you to free your mind and give yourself permission
to create something new. I know your brain will try to convince you that you have
more important things to be worrying about right now, but I want to remind you that
you are in control of those thoughts.

Remember, if you want to share your work on social media, please hashtag
#EssenceOfSurvival so we can all support you and your efforts of healing.

I give myself permission to heal

Day 64

Today, I want you to reflect on the changes you've made in the ways that you speak to yourself. Over this journey, have you learned to be more merciful with yourself, or do you criticize yourself harshly? Do you see any ways you can improve your self-talk? List them below.

Day 65

Today, I want to challenge you to get creative again.

This time, instead of writing a poem, I want you to give yourself permission to dream big and write a short story.

I want you to create a short story of a survivor who has chosen to leave an abusive relationship. Take a moment to write out the challenges they face on their journey to a safer life. Then, I want you to end the story when our character achieves their biggest goal.

I give myself permission to dream big

Day 66

Green Flags

Today, I want to spend some time going over green flags in relationships. Then, I want you to reflect on the information.

- **They know how to communicate effectively:** Communication is key in every relationship. That is why we want to be on the lookout for communication that is honest, open, and respectful. These things are the cornerstones of healthy relationships.
- **They respect your boundaries:** A partner who respects your boundaries and encourages you to maintain them is a huge green flag. Healthy relationships focus on two people having dominion over their own lives.
- **They are empathic and understanding:** Partners who show empathy and compassion when you express sadness or anger help you to create healthy environments for you to establish an emotional connection.
- **They have shared values:** Your partner has similar core values to yours. This allows you to set goals based on your shared values and beliefs.
- **They are dependable and reliable:** You should be able to trust your partner. It is always a green flag when you can trust that your partner is going to do the things they said they would.
- **They encourage individuality:** This might be hard for survivors in the beginning; however, a partner who is not love-bombing you is a good thing. A partner who prioritizes you without changing who you are is a green flag.
- **They know how to resolve conflict in a healthy way:** Disagreements are bound to happen in any relationship; however, in healthy relationships, your partner will come to solutions without forcing their values or opinions on you. They definitely would not include any violence or manipulation.
- **They create spaces that foster intimacy:** Physical and emotional affection are important to bonding. Your partner should prioritize time for this.
- **They are transparent:** A partner who is willing to minimize confusion by being transparent with their emotions and intentions is one of my favorite green flags.

- **They are financially compatible**: A green flag occurs when you can talk to your partner openly about money, goals, spending habits, and responsibilities without a fight.
- **They respect your relationship with your family and friends:** Partners who encourage you to have healthy relationships with others are a green flag. Your partner should encourage you to have a life outside of your relationship with them.
- **They express gratitude and appreciation for you and the things you do for them:** Your partner should be able to vocalize the ways they are grateful for you and the relationship you share together.

Essence of Survival

I didn't cover every green flag; however, hopefully, this helps to set a solid foundation on what a healthy relationship should be built on.

Now, I want you to take some time to reflect on these green flags. Which ones are you looking forward to experiencing most and why?

Day 67

Today, I want to reflect on the day that you decided enough was enough.

For today's journal prompt, I want you to dig deep and put us in the story of the day you realized you could not take the abuse any longer. What were some of the thoughts that had been running through your mind? What feelings were you experiencing during that time? Once you have that information, write it below. Please be sure to include any fears or worries you had at that time, and share if those fears were true.

Day 68

Have you started working with a therapist? If not, why? What is the biggest thing holding you back, and how could you over come that?

If you have started working with someone, what is your favorite part?

Reactive Abuse

Reactive abuse is a term that is used to describe a special type of abuse. Before I get into the full definition of reactive abuse, I want to stress that I am in no way making excuses for abusive behavior; however, this specific type of abuse only comes after a victim has suffered through harsh treatment and reacts in response to how they are treated.

I intentionally put this type of abuse at the very end of the book, and that is because I need you to know and recognize this separately from all of the other types of abuse.

Being in this line of work, it is always so hard when so many things overlap with others. That's why I needed this one to stand out by itself. Earlier, we talked about how abusers will oftentimes shift blame, and I don't want that to be confused with what is happening here. This is not blame-shifting. This type of abuse is the response to the abuse the victim has been on the receiving end of.

When a victim reaches their "breaking point," this is when we can start seeing them choose to fight back. This can be done in various ways. To help you understand how reactive abuse shows up in relationships, let's go over a few examples.

- **Name-Calling:** A victim who is tired of being called out of their name may begin to respond by using the same form of abuse that they don't like to receive.
- **Physical Retaliation:** Tired of being attacked, a victim may decide to fight back. This will result in a physical fight as opposed to the victim being attacked as they have in the past.
- **Threats:** Victims may begin threatening their abuser by saying they will expose their cheating behavior or abusive ways.
- **Property Damage**: Reactive abuse can extend over to property damage. The victim may begin breaking things in response to being tired of the abuse they have been receiving.
- **Accusations:** After being on the receiving end of manipulation tactics, a victim

- **(continued)** may start doing the same behaviors to the other party.
- **Attempts to Leave:** The victim may try to physically leave the situation or end it abruptly.
- **Withholding:** The victim may withhold affection, intimacy, or cooperation as a means of defense.
- **Public Outburst:** Reactive abuse can spill over into public settings as the victim is now tired of silently dealing with the abuse by themselves.
- **Online Retaliation:** The victim may respond to some of the abuse they've suffered by retaliating online. They may share very intimate details about the abuse or the abuser.
- **Seeking Revenge:** In some cases, victims may seek revenge from their abuser. They may do this to harm them physically or to ruin their reputation so the victim can try to regain a feeling of power and control.
- **Blocking Communication:** The victim may abruptly cut off communication from the abuser as a result of relentless harassment.
- **Gaslighting:** After being on the receiving end for a while, the victim may begin to fight back by using some of the same abuse tactics that they have received.

Hopefully, now you can see why I left this until the very end. I did this because I need you to know that without proper healing and knowledge, it is possible that a victim can end up playing the same game with someone else. It is not uncommon for me to see someone go from victim to abuser. I don't want that for you.

Essence of Survival

Now that you have this information, I need you to be honest. Have you ever used any of these reactive abuse tactics, and how did you feel when it was over? You can use the space below to share your story.

Day 70

Yesterday, you briefly wrote about your experience with reactive abuse. Today, I want to dive deeper.

Whenever I am working with clients who have displayed signs of reactive abuse, I always stress to them that if they stay in these types of situations, it is very difficult for untrained eyes to see the abuse they are suffering. Let me clear this up. In court settings and even with law enforcement, many are not required to undergo extensive training on domestic violence. For this reason, they are not always properly equipped to tell the difference between a dysregulated parent and a dysfunctional one.

I realize that up until this point, you have had to suffer a lot of abuse; however, I want to stress that reactive abuse is a temporary relief for a longstanding problem. In fact, it can create more problems for you because then it makes it difficult for someone who may be in a position to help you to do so. If you are constantly going back and forth with your abusive ex, a judge may look at you as the aggressor or the problem instead of the other way around.

Today, I want you to think about some alternative ways that you can respond when you feel triggered. Write out some times that you have been guilty of reactive abuse, and then find an alternative solution that you can try next time.

Day 71

When was the last time that you did something nice for yourself? If you had to think about it, that means that it has been entirely too long.

Remember, self-care is a crucial part of self-love. That is why today, I want to challenge you to do something nice for yourself. I realize that you may not have anything budgeted for this, and that is okay. You don't always have to spend money to show yourself some self-appreciation. Here are a few suggestions:

- **Learn something new:** Head over to the library and grab a book about something you've always wanted to learn about.

- **Get active:** If you are able and your doctor has given you clearance, going to the gym is an amazing way of showing how much you love yourself. Working out provides so many benefits that will always suggest this as one of my personal favorites. (I don't feel this way every day, but because I love myself, I show up even when my mind doesn't want to.)

- **Meditate:** I genuinely appreciate the art of meditation. There is so much power in you that you may not have had the energy to tap into because of abuse. Now that you are free from it, why don't you take some time to slow down your thoughts? Then, when your mind has the freedom to think big, you can visualize a more confident and powerful version of yourself.

- **Connect with Loved Ones:** Abuse has a really nasty way of getting in between our relationships with those we love. As a form of self-care and love, you can pick up the phone and reach out to a loved one. Take a moment to tell them that you love and appreciate them.

- **Decide to Eat Mindfully:** I really love this one. When our emotions are all over the place, it is easy to find comfort in eating too much or too little. You can show yourself that you love yourself by mindfully giving your body what it needs. This could include increasing your water intake, reducing the amount of sugar you consume, or choosing to give your body food that will fuel you for the day.

- **Declutter:** Your physical space is a manifestation of what is going on in the mind. Take charge of your immediate space, and give your mind a sense of control by organizing your things.

Day 72

Without telling me about the abuse you've suffered, what you do for a living, or explaining how many children you have, I want you to write out who you are. When you allow yourself a moment of full introspection, who are you down to your very core?

Day 73

Imagine this: You just inherited a small sum of money, and all of your bills are covered for the rest of the year. You now have $15,000 to plan your dream vacation. I want you to plan out your trip. Be sure to include the destination, how long you plan to stay there, and what you plan to do.

Day 74

Yesterday, you allowed yourself the opportunity to make a decision about money without having to worry about your bills first. I did this intentionally because I know firsthand that when we are out in the wild, fending for our lives, planning a dream vacation is the last thing we are doing. Crazy enough, taking moments to step away from all of our life's problems and visualizing something bigger for ourselves is a great way to give us permission to have hope for more.

Today, give yourself permission to hope for more than you have. What would you want to receive in the next ninety days if you were allowed to have everything you wanted?

Day 75

Today, I want you to list out ten different ways you can compliment yourself on your growth and your vow to safety.

Day 76

Take a moment to reflect on some personal boundaries you've established on this journey. How is this different than before?

I AM BEAUTIFUL

Day 77

Take a moment to reflect on the strategies you have developed to manage triggers and emotional flashbacks.

Day 78

Write about any positive changes you've observed in yourself since leaving the abuse behind.

I RELEASE RELATIONSHIPS THAT VIOLATE MY BOUNDARIES

I am worth it.

Day 79

Keaidy: In therapy, I learned that I use my dark humor as a way to cope with my trauma. Can you think of a time when you have used jokes to lighten the mood? Did it lighten the mood or shift your perspective?

Day 80

Today, I want you to write a list of qualities and characteristics that make you unique and special. Have you always embraced these qualities? How can you build more confidence in these areas?

Day 81

Write out 10 affirmations you can use in your everyday life to help you stay focused on your journey to self-love.

Day 82

Keaidy: As our time together comes to a close, I want you to take a moment to spend a few moments flipping back through this journal. What changes do you see in yourself and in your life?

Day 83

If you could go back in time and offer advice to your past self while in that abusive relationship, what would you say?

Day 84

What are three things that you are thankful for today? It doesn't matter how big or how small. Take a moment to rest in the gratitude you have.

Day 85

Imagine your future self. What does a healthy, thriving, empowered, and successful version of you look like? Then, write out some action steps you can take to make that happen.

Day 86

What exactly does self-empowerment look like to you? How can you help yourself feel more empowered?

Day 87

Boundaries

While I have your attention, let's take a moment to talk about boundaries. In short, boundaries are rules we set for our relationships. Having healthy boundaries for yourself and those you are in a relationship with can protect you from repeating past abusive cycles.

While I can sit here and give you a list of different physical, emotional, mental, and time-related examples you can use to apply boundaries, I believe this would be more effective if you did it.

On the next page, I want you to define your personal boundaries with yourself. From this day forward, how are you allowed to speak to yourself? Are you allowed to call yourself names like silly or fat? Do you give yourself permission to break promises that you make to yourself? Are you allowed to waste your time by procrastinating or creating excuses? These things are important to consider because, moving forward, you set the tone for what is allowed in your life. Life doesn't happen to you. You happen to it.

Today, you are going to set your personal boundaries for this next season of your life. I hope that you realize how important this step is in the rest of your healing journey. This is why I want to strongly urge you to put your all into this next exercise.

Use the space below to dump some ideas out of your brain. Then, on the next page, I need you to re-commit yourself to yourself by setting firm boundaries you plan to adhere to moving forward.

Because I deserve this kind of love..

Day 88

In the next season of your life, how do you plan to love yourself better? What things can you do as a consistent form of love and self-care?

Day 89

Write about a moment when you felt truly empowered. What led to you having these feelings, and how can you recreate it moving forward?

Day 90

On our last day together, I want you to take a moment for you to create your own mantra. What is something that you can commit to speaking over your life daily?

Keaidy: Regardless of what you call them, positive declarations and affirmations hold a lot of power. To help you get started, I've used something that I've personally said over my life.

I don't see problems. Only creative opportunities for solutions.

The Doctor's Orders

You did it! You completed the first ninety days of your healing journey, and I'm so proud of you. More importantly, I hope you are proud of yourself. I know this was not easy. While I gave you a ton of information, there was no way for me to share all of it without overwhelming you. Regardless, you took that information and pushed through each and every day. Good for you.

Before we go our separate ways, I want to take a minute to reflect on the journey we just went on together. Over these last few months, we talked about the complex landscape of domestic violence. We covered the common characteristics of abusers, green flags, boundaries, and the different forms of abuse that can infiltrate our lives. Let's take a brief moment to re-cap some important topics:

You Deserve a Love that Doesn't Hurt.
Oftentimes, we select our partners because the chaos they provided once felt like "home" to us. This means that, at some point, we may have been conditioned to believe that love hurts. As you move forward into this next chapter in your life, I hope you release all of the lies that people spoke about you. You are worthy of great things and deserve a love that doesn't leave you scarred.

You Know the Difference Between Red Flags and Green Ones.
Before you knew what you now know, you chose partners based on the *feelings* they provided to you. Now, you are well aware that sometimes those feelings cannot be trusted. I hope you feel more empowered to make healthier decisions in your love life now that you can consciously recognize red flags. Also, keep in mind that green flags may feel "boring" in the beginning. This is only because you are used to a certain level of toxicity in your previous relationships. Moving forward, let's embrace the fact that a love that is stable, safe, and reliable is the goal. It may take some getting used to, but you deserve it.

You Know the Cycles of Abuse.
We talked about how addicting these cycles can be. Once our brain gets

comfortable with the pattern of something, it tricks us into believing that we are somehow safe because we know what to expect next. Moving forward, I want you to memorize the cycles of abuse and trauma bonds so that you can easily identify if you are in one of those phases again.

You Know the Spectrum of Abuse.

As we discussed, abuse is not always loud and noticeable. We covered physical, sexual, psychological, emotional, spiritual/cultural, financial abuse, and reproductive coercion. We even went into narcissistic abuse and reactive abuse. You should feel empowered to recognize abuse in the future.

You Have a Plan on How to Set Healthy Boundaries with Yourself.

The relationship you have with yourself sets the tone for every other relationship in your life. If you are negative and inconsistent with yourself, you leave the door open to attract others who will be a physical representation of that lack of love that you have within. I want you to continue to build on the boundaries that you set for yourself. As you evolve, allow those boundaries to change also. Hold yourself to such a high standard of love that any other person who comes into your life in the future knows they have to love you with that same amount of respect and passion.

You Know Self-Care is an Essential Part of Self-Love.

You cannot pour from an empty cup. You cannot take care of others when you are riding on fumes. As you navigate this next season of your life, I hope that you continue to find reasons to pour into yourself the way that you have done to others. Find a new love of life. Start a new hobby or go after something you've only dreamed of. This is your time to do that. The more that you give to yourself, the more you'll be able to give and receive love from others.

You Know How Trauma Impacts Your Body and Brain.

You may have been living with symptoms of how uncomfortable your trauma has left you. Maybe you are riddled with constant anxiety, or the impact is now showing up in the physical form through sickness and pain. Please take this information with you and provide it to your doctors. Having this information will help them help you during this time.

You are Empowered to Make Better Decisions for Yourself.

I recognize that you may still be trying to find stable ground after getting out of that abusive relationship; however, through this time, you've acquired a ton of information that should leave you feeling empowered to make better decisions moving forward. In addition, you should hold more compassion and empathy for what you've been through. Allowing yourself the freedom to show yourself some grace is going to help you as you transition into this next season. You did the best you could with the information you had at the time. You cannot change it; those experiences have helped fuel you into the resilient person you are today.

You Have Established a Habit of Consistently Showing up for Yourself.

For the last 90 days, you've honored your vow to yourself! That's a major accomplishment. You should be proud of yourself. Now, you should continue to build on to this habit with another journal.

And now... your final Doctor's Order.

As my final send-off, I want you to live your best life. The first couple of years may be challenging as you step into a different version of yourself, but keep showing up anyway. Greater is coming later. Then, when you're ready, I want you to turn around and help someone else on their healing journey. Encourage a friend to commit themselves to this ninety-day challenge or volunteer at a center that helps domestic violence survivors. Regardless of what you decide to do, do something.

Dr. Allanah Roberts-Headley

About Dr. Allanah Roberts-Headley

Dr. Allanah Roberts-Headley is a dedicated mental health professional and accomplished educator deeply committed to empowering individuals on their journey toward healing and self-discovery. With her extensive background as a licensed mental health counselor and a distinguished doctor in counselor education, she brings a wealth of experience and expertise to clinical mental health.

As a professor at a leading Florida university, Dr. Roberts-Headley focuses on instilling knowledge, compassion, and resilience in her students, shaping the next generation of mental health advocates. Her dedication to the field extends beyond academia, as she is also a passionate motivational speaker and advocate for mental health awareness.

Dr. Roberts-Headley loves to connect with her readers. You can follow her practice on Instagram at @essence_of_the_mind.

About Keaidy Bennett

Keaidy Bennett, an author, activist, and CEO of LexxiKhan Presents Publishing, hails from the vibrant land of Honduras. She presently resides in Orlando, FL, with her three children.

As a gifted storyteller, Keaidy Bennett pens the compelling urban fiction series **Charge it to the Game**, unveiling the harsh realities of chasing fast money. As a speaker, she motivates entrepreneurs and storytellers to leave their legacy in print for the world to see.

Beyond the pages, Keaidy stands as a fierce activist, particularly advocating for post-abuse support for survivors of domestic violence. Drawing from her own trials, she offers a light, empowering others to heal and thrive.

Follow Keaidy Bennett's literary world, explore her latest releases, and connect with her at **lexxikhanpresents.com/kdb**. Share your thoughts, for your words might inspire her next literary masterpiece. Join Keaidy on a transformative journey where resilience and empowerment will always prevail.

You can follow Keaidy on Instagram at @akawords

www.ingramcontent.com/pod-product-compliance
Lightning Source LLC
Chambersburg PA
CBHW041115120626
46547CB00019B/2712